FEAR NOT!

— UNLEASH —
THE CONQUEROR
WITHIN —

AMI THOMSON

WestBow
PRESS®
A DIVISION OF THOMAS NELSON
& ZONDERVAN

WestBow Press books may be ordered through booksellers or by contacting:

WestBow Press
A Division of Thomas Nelson & Zondervan
1663 Liberty Drive
Bloomington, IN 47403
www.westbowpress.com
844-714-3454

Editor: Jeanette Windle

ISBN: 978-1-6642-0235-1 (sc)
ISBN: 978-1-6642-0237-5 (hc)
ISBN: 978-1-6642-0236-8 (e)

Library of Congress Control Number: 2020915468

Print information available on the last page.

WestBow Press rev. date: 9/24/2020

DEDICATION

To Jesus. You are worthy of it all. You are my resurrection and life, savior, redeemer, and healer. To the person of the Holy Spirit. My best friend, ever present help, comforter, counselor, wisdom, and power. Life with you is glorious!

CONTENTS

Fear Not! Unleash the Conqueror Within

> *"They triumphed over him [the enemy] by the blood of the Lamb and by the word of their testimony; they did not love their lives so much as to shrink from death."*
>
> REVELATIONS 12:11

If someone had told me a few years ago that today I would be sharing a success strategy of hope, promise, blessing, and a future, I would never have believed it. At that time, I was in a death-trap of panic attacks, grueling pain, and hopelessness. What God revealed to me in my darkest hour is so rich, the transformation he effected in my life so powerful, I still can hardly grasp that it is real.

We all have a life story to tell, and our current life is a direct reflection of the perspective we've learned from our past life—i.e., our history. For example, if you are blessed to be living a life of joy, peace, and promise of a great future, then somewhere along the way you've learned to maintain a perspective of joy, peace, and expectancy even in the face of pain and disappointment. Maybe you learned this from a parent or grandparent. Maybe you learned it through personal experiences with Jesus Christ.

Or maybe your life is not one of such victory and joy. Maybe you are like so many of the rest of us, struggling instead with secret, not-so-desirable areas in our lives we'd rather keep hidden. Negative strongholds such as anxiety, aggression, insecurity, addictions, eating disorders, self-injuring, perfectionism, obsessive compulsion, and/or depression leave us feeling overwhelmed because we feel powerless to do anything about them.

What we fail to recognize is that these characteristics may just be the tip of our internal iceberg. What lies beneath the surface are layers of past experiences that have inflicted injury, trauma, and pain. And it is to this submerged iceberg that fear finds ways to attach itself.

Fear is the culminating, binding factor that exacerbates our negative strongholds because those strongholds are based on and birthed out of fear. Like an unwanted intruder at a masquerade ball, fear shows up in a myriad of disguises, eliciting behavior that is not our true nature or our real identity but defensive adaptations. Today's culture of self-help and self-esteem tells us to just accept our fear-derived characteristics and learn to cope or co-exist with them. But that is not what God's Word teaches us in the Bible.

So here is my question for you. Does fear have you pushed into a corner of doubt, dread, insecurity, depression, anxiety, addictions, and/or disorder? Have you felt so hard-kicked in the gut by trauma, distress, oppression that you find yourself lying flat on the floor, flailing around and sucking wind to get your breath back?

That was me less than five years ago. My own personal history was one giant flimsy house of cards. From the outside, my life looked great. But it was unstable at best, built on a fractured foundation of fear. The walls I'd built up for my own personal security and self-preservation were fragile, faulty, full of holes. No amount of self-help books, expensive therapy, or anti-depressants could help me. Believe me, I tried it all! Nothing and no one but God himself could help me. If God did not rescue me, I knew I would surely die.

Fear Not! Unleash the Conqueror Within was birthed from real-life traumas, failures, and need for an identity realignment that threatened my sanity, hope, destiny, and very existence. Like a bear who'd remained hibernating in her cave far past springtime, I awoke to the realization that God's promises in his Word had been falling empty and without nourishment to the ground. Something in my life was very wrong. Angry and starving for truth, I determined that either God was a liar, or I'd been deceived into believing I was a powerless victim of circumstances.

In desperation, I put God's Word to test. Cocooned in God's very presence and promises, I consented to the ministry of the Holy Spirit, who touched me physically and breathed life into decaying and dead hope, relationships, purpose, and destiny. Soon I began to see the ruined, hopeless circumstances in which I was living surrender to God's sovereign promises. Little by little, I dared to believe, dared to hope, and dared to dream with God of my identity, destiny, power, and authority as an inheritance-carrying child of the Most High God through the redemption of his Son Jesus Christ.

What I discovered is that our Father God does not want us crippled with fear. That's not the spirit he has given us. When we can understand how loved and empowered we are right now today because of God's Spirit within us, we shatter the power of the spirit of fear and intimidation and unleash the more-than-conqueror that is inside us as God's children. As God's heirs. This is the best news ever. Especially for those of us who are crushed and weighed down in panic attacks, pain, or debilitating depression.

Now don't get me wrong. I'm not claiming to have arrived at a place of perfection. Not by a long shot! But when I look back today over the last few years of my life, I am amazed to see peace, joy, and a whole lot of great expectation for the future. My change in perspective occurred miraculously despite horrendous, disastrous circumstances.

God did not create the disastrous circumstances. But he did use them to offer me an opportunity for transformation. An opportunity to participate with the miraculous. Choosing to participate with the miraculous doesn't always produce instant results. There are deep, dark valleys and refining fire we sometimes need to walk through before the transformation and miraculous can even begin. For me, that transitional valley was so long, so hard, and so painful I couldn't see the other side. My only joy and hope in that bone-dry, scalding-hot chasm was found in worshipping my heavenly Father for his faithfulness and goodness.

But while at the time it felt that hard valley of transformation would go on and on forever, as I look back across it now in my rear-view mirror, I can see how God used the depth and breadth of pain, trauma, and fear to propel me forward into the destiny he had for me. For the past two years now, God has been encouraging me to trace the lineage of fear through my life, then untangle that fear and uproot it like a gardener removing a strangling vine out of a garden.

Tracing fear is hard work. It is also painful because it tugs at painful memories. It pulls on hidden pasts and yanks up mistakes I'd much prefer to leave covered and hidden. But the exercise has been more than worth the pain. Freedom is well worth the price!

This in turn has led to the writing of this book as God laid it on my heart to share with others the same miracle-working promises from God's Word and the power of the Person of Jesus Christ, who became my hiding place and rescue in the darkest hours. In the following pages, we will walk together through a practical step-by-step guide for implementing and applying God's Word to work on our behalf and transform us into becoming more-than-a-conqueror according to God's promises.

This book is intended to be a working journal. It is your action plan and your success strategy to total knock-out victory in Jesus Christ. Proceed at your own pace. Return to it as often as you need. Inside its pages, journal your battle. Highlight anything and everything that speaks to you. Add your notes to the portions of your battle plan you know will need revisiting.

Together with Christ, hidden in Christ, you can create history. His-story! The story of a victorious daily life that reverberates your Savior's passionate love for you and magnifies his power in you, all for his glory. Document your victory. Then you will have a testament of your testimony—that pivotal point in your life when *His* story becomes *your* story.

It is my prayer that every single person reading this who may be struggling with fear, insecurity, anxiety, depression, addiction, or hopelessness, regardless of who or where in life you may be today, will receive every promise in this book. Not a single one of us can ever be good enough or worthy enough to receive God's amazing love, mercy, and power. But we can all be recipients and participants of a lavish inheritance of peace, hope, and joy because of Jesus's finished work at the cross.

Join me, and together we will learn to stand up, rise up, push fear back into its corner, knock it right out of the ring, and keep it defeated forever!

"Consenting to God's perfect plan through the power of the blood and resurrection of Christ produces all the healing, power, and authority we need to be more than conquerors in THIS life!"

—Ami Thomson

CHAPTER ONE

LEARNED FEAR

*"The reason the Son of God appeared was
to destroy the works of the devil."*

1 JOHN 3:8 (ESV)

I was born in Montana in early 1972. From what I've heard, I believe that at the time of my birth we were a happy Christian family. Momma and Dad were both from the south, so we had no extended family in Montana. But I'm told we had a wonderful community of loving Christian friends.

As to immediate family, I was the youngest of five children. My three older sisters were born close together, just a year between the oldest and second sister and two years between her and the third. My only brother was born four years after the three girls. Then I came along about eighteen months later.

My dad had felt a calling to ministry since high school, but in his second year of seminary he was told by professors and other superiors that he didn't have the spiritual depth to be a minister. So he changed colleges and graduated as a schoolteacher. Though not a credentialed minister, he did exercise his calling as a preacher during our time in Montana along with teaching school.

Then shortly after my birth, we moved back down south to Texas to be near aging grandparents. Our new home was a vacant church parsonage with two bedrooms and one bath. After the move, our family never relocated the happy we'd experienced in our Montana home. We'd moved from a place of beauty and grace to a place of judgement and fear.

This began shortly after our relocation when my parents became involved in a church that emphasized teachings from the Shepherding Movement. Much can be found on the internet about this movement, but in brief, each man like my dad was assigned a "shepherd", who watched over and mentored their particular flock of "sheep." The movement was organized in a classic pyramid business model where each "shepherd" in turn was the "sheep" of another "shepherd" higher up the pyramid. Orders and decrees were issued from the top down, and every "sheep" was required to submit absolutely to their own "shepherd," as they in turn must submit to the shepherd above them.

You can imagine the possibilities for abuse of power. The mentoring and accountability elements also included scrutinizing and critiquing the "sheep" for flaws and imperfections, which were in turn to be pointed out and reported on to others. That alone should be cause for unrest since no one needs to be constantly scrutinized and criticized. For my dad, this became a major fear factor, and he began experiencing great anxiety. Soon he began hearing tormenting inner voices that constantly accused and berated him, causing great fear.

Eventually the Shepherding Movement was exposed for the cult it had become and was denounced by Christian leadership across both charismatic and non-charismatic denominations. Men within the movement's leadership even apologized for the damage caused to their followers. But though the movement largely petered out, within our own home its fundamental teachings were still upheld. One of those elements was absolute submission to the head of the household—the husband/father. The end result was a terribly twisted legalistic, dogmatic spirit of religious condemnation that infected my parents' hearts, clouded their thinking, and inflicted tremendous pain on the family.

Let me make clear that my earthly father is a man of God who served in ministry for many, many years, and still does to this day. He is not the same person today as he was in my childhood. By the grace of God our relationship has been restored. I can also testify honestly that today I am free of bitterness and anger, though remaining in that freedom still requires a conscious choice at times. But God has called me to write my story in order to loosen and undo the works of our enemy, Satan, including the heavy, binding chains of fear. And when my heavenly Abba, or Father, calls me to do something, I delight in obeying—period! In doing so, I endeavor to share my story to the best of my ability in a spirit of power and love that speaks truth while still endeavoring to honor my earthly father.

Getting back to that story, fear was a constant member of our household for as long as I can remember. By the age of two, I understood terror only too well. I was terrified of people—what they might do or say to me. I was afraid of talking for fear I might say something wrong or be shut down. Mostly, I was very, very afraid of my dad. All five of us children were.

So What's the Big Deal with Fear?

Let me make clear that fear in and of itself is not a negative characteristic but an adaptive behavior crafted by God as part of our genetic makeup. In fact, the Bible references the "fear of the Lord [God]" as the beginning of wisdom (Proverbs 9:10), and followers of God are often commanded in Scripture to fear God (Deuteronomy 6:24, Psalm 34:9). Conversely, a main characteristic the Bible lists of an ungodly people who have turned to evil is that they stopped fearing God (Psalm 36:1, Romans 3:18). We will talk more in-depth later about what an appropriate fear of God entails and how it differs from gut-punching, breath-snatching, agonizing, debilitating terror that makes it impossible to function in our daily lives.

But going back to a basic definition, the positive value of fear is that it alerts us of potential threats so we can determine how to handle situations we encounter. During such scenarios, our brains instinctively makes decisions to get out of the situation, stay and defend ourselves, or simply hold still and wait for the danger to get past us. This is commonly described as our "fight, flight, or freeze" instinct. Fear is a useful tool in helping us avoid and survive dangerous situations.

Unfortunately, fear is a slippery slope. It can become disproportionate to our normal survival instinct, particularly when it is the aftermath of an injury or trauma. This pain-derived fear tends to stay with us long-term by embedding itself in our reasoning and decision-making. For example, we lose a precious loved one far too early so we become afraid we might lose other loved ones prematurely or even die prematurely ourselves.

Which brings us to a more in-depth discussion of fear. We've already mentioned the positive aspect of fear as a protective mechanism against danger as well as the biblically mandated "fear of the Lord," which we will discuss later. Another type of fear is what behavioralists term "instinctive fear," which is literally programmed into our DNA. Scientists have narrowed down two fears that we are born with—the fear of falling and the fear of loud or sudden noises, i.e., the acoustic "startle" reflex which anyone who has been around infants will recognize. These two primal fears are again God's natural way to help us survive infancy. Virtually all other fears—specifically, negative, damaging fears—are either *learned* or *inherited*.

Learned Fear

Learned fears come from people, situations, and circumstances within our environment. For instance, as a little boy my older brother touched a hot vent on the roof of the little shanty house behind the church where we lived in Longview, Texas. He shouldn't have been on the roof at all, but that's another story for another day. His little finger bubbled up with a huge, horribly painful blister. Momma was angry, Dad was sheepish, and big brother was screaming. He learned a healthy respect for hot things, but so did baby sister—that's me—from witnessing the uproar.

We may also witness a parent, siblings, other family members, or friends modeling fear towards snakes, spiders, heights, crowded rooms, speaking to groups of people, and so on. The more often we see a fear displayed and the more significant the one modeling this fear is to us, the more likely we are to "learn" or adopt those same fears as our own.

Other learned fears are those resulting from personally hurtful experiences and circumstances that leave a lasting impression. The loss of a child, sibling, parent, or other close family member causes intense grief. Betrayal in a close relationship, such as a marriage, shatters trust. Each of these, if not fully dealt with, can lead to ongoing fear as can painful disappointment, rejection, and other traumas.

Let's discuss trauma for a moment. The majority of us have likely experienced some kind of trauma in our lives. That doesn't necessarily mean we are saddled with burdens of emotional baggage and destined to develop fear issues. But young children and adolescents are far more likely than adults to develop trauma-related and fear-based behaviors such as addiction, eating disorders, self-injuring, mood disorders like anxiety and depression, along with correlating high blood pressure, ulcers, psoriasis, and so on. This is especially true if the trauma is repeated and there is no relief or support available.

Even a one-time trauma can have devastating effects. A small child sexually molested at four years of age may internalize and even bury the event from memory. But as the child enters adolescence and adult life, the damage of insecurity can affect a healthy development of close relationships and even intimacy with a spouse. Those of us who experienced repeated, unavoidable physical, sexual, and/ or emotional abuse as children are, sadly, prime candidates for developing fear-based behaviors. Likewise, those who have experienced being bullied, manipulated, humiliated, rejected, and discriminated against at home, school, or in work environments.

Fear, depression, and anxiety disorders have become an epidemic in western society. According to the CDC (see *Psychiatric News*, September 15, 2017, www.psychnews.psychiatryonline.org), between 2011 and 2014 alone, approximately one in nine Americans of all ages reported taking at least one antidepressant medication in the past month. Three decades prior, less than one in fifty Americans did. The use of antidepressants increases with age with nearly nineteen percent of adults sixty-five years and older taking them in contrast to an earlier study from 1988 to 1994, when only three percent of older adults were taking antidepressants.

Activity A: Known Fears

Before we go on, let's take a moment and document the known fears that cycle and spin through our minds and lives. These can include fears adopted from others (like seeing my brother burn himself) or resulting from our own past traumas and/or injuries that have left physical and emotional scars. Here are a just few to get our brains thinking. Fear of dying (self, child, or others). Fear of flying. Anxiety when driving. Fear of water/swimming. Fear of speaking up in front of people. Fear of failure. Fear of rejection. Fear of falling short of expectations. Fear of intimacy or commitment. Fear of being alone. And so on.

Take your time. Over the next several days or months, return to this section and document more as they come to mind. If you run out of room here, consider journaling in a separate notebook.

_____

_____

_____

_____

_____

_____

_____

_____

_____

CHAPTER TWO

INHERITED FEAR

*"The God of peace will soon crush Satan under your
feet. The grace of our Lord Jesus be with you."*

ROMANS 16:20

"So, what's the big deal?" we might say. "Life stinks sometimes.
Everyone experiences hurt and fear in life. It's unavoidable
sometimes, right?"

That may be correct if we view life through this world's lens.
Here's the major issue with learned fears. We can easily get caught
in a vicious loop, replaying over and over moments of injury, pain,
guilt, blame, and shame, the events leading up to those moments, and
the punitive aftermath. In situations of extreme stress and pain like
PTSD (Post Traumatic Stress Disorder) these moments are referred
to as flashbacks. A noise, smell, similar environment, or sometimes
nothing at all can trigger these horrible instant replays in agonizing
detail.

As our minds relive these traumatic events, we ask ourselves
logical but typically fruitless questions to help our brains find some
reasonable rationale. How did this happen? Who could do such a
thing? What did I do to deserve this? What could I have done to
prevent this? Why, why, why?

Does that blame game sound familiar? In these questions, we
are trying to make sense of the injury so that we can move on and,
most importantly, ensure we never allow ourselves to be vulnerable
to such an injury again. The problem is that this can lead to what I
like to call "stinkin' thinkin'."

I call it that because this kind of thinking isn't the reasoning
power God gave us. Getting stuck in a loop of play, rewind, and
repeat can open a window of opportunity for a spirit of fear to enter

the scene. We'll discuss the spirit of fear further after we talk about inherited fear.

Inherited Fear

Inherited fear is a fear tendency that has been handed down from someone in our family, often over multiple generations. This scenario is far less recognized because it isn't as widely understood or taught. But you might hear someone say of another, "Well, it's only natural. Her mother was a real worrier too." Or comment about a mutual acquaintance, "He's just like his daddy. That man just hated social gatherings and crowds."

Many other tendencies can be passed down as well, such as alcoholism, drug abuse, abusive behavior, sexual promiscuity/ addictions, and so on. Inherited fear can hide out for a long time, corroding our confidence and ultimately leading us into delaying or even short-selling the plan and purpose God has for us. It can bind us in self-doubt and drag us through "what if" scenarios until we are frozen with analysis paralysis. It is an incumbrance that prevents us from being all that we are called to be. Take a few minutes to reflect on your life. If you experience numerous regrets because you didn't take greater risks going for your goals, then it's likely due to this type of fear.

My own dad had inherited fear from previous generations and from a very young age lived with constant fear and feelings of unworthiness. While he'd been given opportunity to preach in Montana, he hadn't been in Texas, and I believe his greatest fear was that he'd be judged imperfect and inadequate both as a minister and as a man of God.

We lived in the church parsonage for a total of six and a half years. Dad worked various jobs, but steady, good-paying employment was hard for him to find. With seven mouths to feed, I remember some very lean, hungry years.

We eventually moved from Texas to a rural area of Arkansas.

Our rental home was tucked on a dirt road between wooded areas, cow pastures, ponds, and one very smelly chicken factory across the pasture behind our house. Dad taught at the local school for a while. He was also hired to gather eggs manually at the chicken factory, at which the rest of us all pitched in. He finally landed a decent-paying job on a construction site.

During all this, Dad was given opportunities to preach at several churches and eventually became the pastor of a tiny, old church in a tiny, old town about thirty minutes from our home. He held that position for three years while continuing to work in construction. Then we moved again to a town in Arkansas of about five thousand.

There Dad continued to work the construction job for a time, then became janitor at the local Wal-Mart, where he worked for many years. Later he became the janitor for First Baptist Church. He always remained involved in ministry—as substitute pastor, interim pastor, elder, etc. Along with other Christian friends, he eventually started a small church that held together until my siblings and I were all gone from home and my momma had passed away.

In all of this, his wife and five children were a direct reflection of my father's religious achievement, so he demanded that we be perceived always as the perfect family with perfectly behaved children. This meant instant, submissive obedience. We children were under constant scrutiny for imperfection, whether real or perceived. The penalty for falling short was excruciatingly painful, both physically and emotionally. Discipline was not administered out of love but intimidation, control, and often anger with frequent and prolonged application of "the rod." We children were often wrongly accused with no idea what we were being punished for. Momma did step in occasionally when the accusations were blatantly false. But I think she felt powerless to defend us.

The unrelenting punishment instilled great physical and emotional pain in all five of us children while the harsh spirit in which the punishment was meted out left us feeling rejected and unworthy of our dad's love. As a Christian family, we were supposed to know that God is love, unconditionally. We did not. The very concept of an unconditionally loving, caring heavenly Father was unfathomable to us because we'd never seen such fatherly love demonstrated. Perhaps you can identify with this.

This "discipline" continued until we children became teenagers, too big or old to spank. I remember one day when I was about thirteen years old and beginning to develop into a young lady. I had asked my dad if I could go to a school dance. I was disappointed if not particularly surprised when he said no. But I made no attempt to argue further.

Instead, I headed into our home's only bathroom, where I could see my mom touching up her makeup. I wanted to complain to her, though I knew she wouldn't overturn my dad's decision. But I also needed to use the facilities. With five females in our family of seven, at least one or more of us was typically in the bathroom, so we were well accustomed to using the facilities while another sister or our momma was fixing their hair or makeup.

I closed the bathroom door behind me, not realizing my dad had followed. I was using the facilities when Dad pushed open the door, "the rod" already in hand. My closing the door on him was an act of defiance, he informed me. Now I would be punished. Momma sighed, rolled her eyes, but said nothing.

As Dad entered the bathroom, white-hot waves of terror and anguish washed over me. The knowledge of what was coming played out across the movie screen of my mind like a too-familiar horror scene. First, the guilty verdict and sentencing. It didn't matter that I was once again being wrongly accused. Then the main event—the spanking. This would include the humiliating bent-over position in which I would be forced to endure the excruciatingly painful torrent of his rage until he was satisfied sufficient correction had been given to what he referred to as my "strong will" or "rebellious spirit." Then would come the final act of injustice— always my dad's justification for another unjustifiable punishment—which was his parting admonishment to "never let this happen again."

But this time something in me snapped. My mind screamed out,

"ENOUGH! I've had enough of this! No more! I'm not going down without a fight!"

"What are you saying, crazy girl?" my brain immediately answered back. "Have you lost your mind?!"

The victim in me added a plea for survival. "Don't resist. Just go quietly. Maybe if you are submissive, there will be mercy."

But now my inner warrior was shouting, "You tell him, girl! NO MORE forever!"

I chose to listen to my inner warrior. After all, what had I to lose? If I was going to receive a brutal beating anyway, I might as well put up a good fight. With fingernails dug in and teeth clenched, I clung to the doorframe with all my might. My voice sounded shaky and tear-filled, but my words held absolute conviction as I said, "Dad, you can ground me for the rest of my life. You can punish me any other way. But you will never do *this* to me EVER AGAIN!"

And he never did. But the constant critical scrutinizing, disapproval, and judgment never left our home. All of us, Momma included, felt that we fell short of Dad's esteem, approval, and love. While I recognize now it was a lie from the devil, I grew up feeling that I was an imposition, an inconvenience, a disposable dissatisfaction to my earthly father.

Activity B: Inherited/Historical Fear

We've listed our known fears. Now let's go deeper and identify which of those fears are inherited and the relationship/person from whom they derived. Go back into your lineage as far as you can trace the same fear. For instance, I learned fear of not measuring up as well as fear or rejection from my dad, who in turn learned it from his parents. Include as much detail as you can.

Again, you may want to consider journaling in a separate notebook so that you can come back over the next several days or months to document more details as they come to mind. Don't take shortcuts on this activity. You are documenting your healing story!

_____

_____

_____

_____

_____

_____

_____

_____

_____

_____

CHAPTER THREE

SPIRIT OF FEAR

"For God has not given us a spirit of fear but one
of power, love, and sound judgement."
2 TIMOTHY 1:7; CHRISTIAN STANDARD BIBLE

Inherited fear that has been handed down over a generation or more probably has a spirit root to it. What does that mean? The apostle Paul in writing to his disciple Timothy made a powerful statement (see Timothy 1:7 above) that has become one of God's promises I come back to again and again.

There are two points about fear this verse makes clear. First, it can become a spirit dwelling within us. Without being spooky, this means that a fearful way of thinking or looking at the world around us has anchored itself within our mind and emotions (that part of a person often termed the soul).

More significantly—and the good news in this verse!—is that this spirit of fear does not come from God. Quite the opposite. When Jesus was teaching his disciples how to pray, he told them:

> If you then, who are evil, know how to give good
> gifts to your children, how much more will the
> heavenly Father give the Holy Spirit to those who
> ask him! (Luke 11:13, English Standard Version)

Even flawed earthly parents want to give good gifts to their children. How much more a loving heavenly Father. A loving heavenly Father doesn't give fear to his children any more than he would offer them a poisonous snake. Instead, he gives the Holy Spirit. The outflow of that gift is an inner spirit (i.e., our mind and emotions) that instead of fear is characterized by power, love, and sound judgement, or wisdom.

In fact, the word translated "power" in 1 Timothy 1:7 is the Greek word *dunamis* from which we derive the English word for dynamite. It isn't power in the sense of authority or lording over others, but the explosive, miracle-working, resurrecting power that characterized the life of Jesus Christ during his time on this earth. As the apostle Paul told Timothy, it is God's intention that we wield this same wonder-working power in our earthly lives.

We'll talk more about that later when we learn how to become more-than-conquerors in banishing our fears. But based on these scriptures, we can recognize that fear, oppression, and depression are not part of God's plan and purpose for our lives. So where does the spirit of fear come from?

Simply put, just as God gives us the good gifts of power, love, and sound judgement, it is God's enemy Satan, the evil one, the devil, who bestows the spirit of fear on anyone willing to accept it. What is Satan's purpose in doing this? Because he is in a battle with God for our lives. For our souls. Using the analogy of himself as the Good Shepherd and us as his sheep, Jesus described Satan's goal.

> The thief does not come except to steal, and to kill, and to destroy. I have come that they may have life, and that they may have it more abundantly. (John 10:10, NKJV)

Satan is both a thief and a liar, and he fights dirty. He will do everything he can to steal your identity as God's child. To kill the spirit of power, love, and sound judgement within you. To destroy your peace and joy. Like a hungry lion, he is always looking for one more person to gobble up, as the apostle Peter warned.

> Be sober-minded; be watchful. Your adversary the devil prowls around like a roaring lion, seeking someone to devour. (1 Peter 5:8, ESV)

And fear is Satan's number one go-to weapon. Not a single human on this planet is immune. It is not only a highly effective weapon but easily disguised and recyclable, rather like a nasty virus that sneaks into our body at one point of weakness, then begins to spread out and hijack healthy parts. Similarly, a spirit of fear will sneakily overtake a scenario or two and then try to trespass into other scenarios.

For example, maybe you've witnessed a particularly nasty accident on a specific section of interstate so now you are nervous about driving down that section. You keep having mental replays of the accident so you begin taking more indirect, less efficient routes regardless of how this delays your trip. Over time, you begin to feel nervous about driving on any other road with multiple lanes of traffic moving in the same direction like the turnpike, interstate, and state roads. You begin avoiding major traffic arteries of any kind. This spreads to feeling jumpy in heavily populated parking lots and so on. Before long you've quit driving altogether to avoid the mental images of car accidents and the constant discomfort of fear.

How Does a Spirit of Fear Enter?

At this point you might ask: "Wouldn't a person know if they had a spirit of fear?"

Not always. Satan is a master of disguise (2 Corinthians 11:14). He will camouflage his voice with your inner voice so that it sounds like you're speaking to yourself. He whispers negative thoughts about ourselves and others that bring about insecurity, intimidation, inferiority, bitterness, anger, hatred, and so on. Our daily environment normalizes the stress, anxiety, and depression associated with fear to the point that we expect it, accept it, and navigate life with it as though fear is just one of our body parts.

But that spirit of fear is NOT you! And don't forget what Jesus the Good Shepherd promised his sheep in the above passage. Satan's goal is to steal, kill, destroy, and devour. But Jesus came that we might have life and have it more abundantly (John 10:10).

So how does that spirit of fear creep in? Fear can creep in through a traumatic event like an accident, injury, trauma, abuse, humiliation, or sin to name a few. Another opening for fear is our reasoning and thinking. What we meditate on offers a window of opportunity. When that window is left open even just a crack, the spirit of fear can creep in. Remember the stinkin' thinkin' we mentioned in the previous section? When we get stuck in that stinkin' thinkin' loop, it can look something like the following:

- Relive the trauma
- Assimilate information
- Deliberate justification
- Avoidance planning
- Repeat

When a loop like this gets stored in our emotional and mental processing, it's because we've chosen to camp out in the valley instead of walking through it as King David describes in Psalm 23.

> Even though I walk through the valley of the shadow of death, I will fear no evil, for you are with me; your rod and your staff protect and comfort me. (Psalms 23:4)

Psalm 23, also known as the Good Shepherd's Psalm, is a depiction of us as a sheep following our Good Shepherd. This may take us down into dark, gloomy valleys. But notice that the psalm tells us we are to walk *through* the valley of the shadow of death, not make it our base camp. And even in the midst of the valley, we don't need to accept a spirit of fear because our heavenly Good Shepherd is with us. He watches over, protects, and comforts us.

The devil has a great success rate with this age-old tactic. But we are going to eradicate fear and keep that lying, defeated devil underneath Jesus's feet—and therefore underneath OUR feet! Amen? But I'm getting ahead of myself again.

Activity C: Fear Behaviors

We've listed our learned fears and our inherited fears. Now let's take a moment and document as well any recurring behaviors that are the consequence of fear. For example, self-medicating (alcohol, pain medications, etc.). Self-injuring. Eating disorders. Sleeping disorders like insomnia. Stress or anxiety disorders, including panic attacks. General reactions such as being easily intimidated, confrontational, hot-tempered, frequently angry about annoyances in life, including other people. Habitually avoiding confrontation. Recurring or persistent depression (list also what you think you are depressed about).

Again, take your time. Over the next several days or months, return to this section (or your auxiliary journal) and document more as they come to mind.

_____

_____

_____

_____

_____

_____

_____

_____

_____

CHAPTER FOUR

FEAR OF THE LORD

*"Fathers, do not provoke your children,
lest they become discouraged."*

COLOSSIANS 3:21 (ESV)

In my case, I'd left the window of opportunity wide open for a spirit of fear to creep in. And fear left unhealed begets anger. Anger in turn begets hate.

By the time I was fifteen years old, I absolutely loathed my dad. I hated the atmosphere in our home, especially when he was present. I hated always being poor and doing without. I hated not being seen or heard or considered valuable. And I blamed him entirely. Sometimes I even fantasied about killing him until I realized how upset Momma would probably be, which blew my daydream. I fed the flames of anger and hatred until one day around the age of sixteen when I had a very different kind of dream.

To this day I don't know if I'd actually drifted off to sleep, but the vision or dream I had was and still is crystal-clear. Our evening meal had been cleared away, but Dad remained sitting at the table as he often did. This evening he was looking through an envelope of printed-out photos, commenting on people and events in the photos. But he had the details wrong.

"Umm, Dad, I think that's actually so-and-so," I gently attempted to correct him. "And I'm pretty sure we were at such-and-such a place."

"No, that is so-and-so and it was at such-and-such!" Dad argued back angrily.

I saw the fury in his eyes at being challenged and defied by his daughter. Typically, the fury would burn for a short time. Then would come the blank look of resolute action, the point of no return.

Whatever happened from this point on was absolutely going to be my worst nightmare. But instead of backing down with characteristic acquiescence, I held his gaze and argued back. Somehow in my dream, I felt it was important to stand up to his anger and tell the truth, no matter what happened next.

Sure enough, my enraged dad grabbed my arm and attempted to lead me away to "deal" with me. The dream skipped over any details of the physical altercation. The next scene showed Dad lying flat on his back on the floor, unconscious. Apparently there'd been a wrestling match and I'd won. Yay, me! Justice at last!

Then the vision took a dark turn. An unseen hand or force lifted Dad's shirt above his chest, then traced a circle on his chest. The tracing wasn't in pen or colored marker. It had been cut with an unseen blade, and now the cut filled in black-red with Dad's blood. Next, to my shock and horror, the unseen power sliced a pentagram inside the circle.

"What could this mean?" I asked myself in dismay.

The response that came to me was that my hatred had the power to keep my dad in bondage and oppression. He was allowing the enemy to operate in his life in more ways than one, in particular when it came to disciplining his children. My hatred and refusal to forgive him was contributing to that bondage and oppression.

Overwhelmed with grief and urgency, I sat straight up in bed. Fully awake now, I sobbed for mercy. Mercy from God to make a way for Dad to escape. Mercy for God to do the impossible and help me forgive my dad. And mercy from God to help me remain in that forgiveness.

God is faithful to grant mercy and grace when his children cry out to him. And through God's mercy and grace, I committed myself from that night forward to remain faithful in forgiving my dad. This wasn't always easy. There were many times—and still are—when persevering in that forgiveness has required a deliberate choice. But there is *power* in forgiveness. Oh, the freedom, the liberty, the joy it brings when I choose to remain in a state of forgiveness! I have no power in and of myself to forgive, much less to continue forgiving. Only the grace of God enables and empowers forgiveness for atrocities and injuries that cut to the core.

Fear of the Lord

Before we go on talking about how to deal with the wrong kinds of fear, let's just stop and take some time to define clearly what the fear of the Lord, or fear of God, means. After all, the Bible tells us to fear God. Jesus himself told his disciples when sending them out to announce his kingdom:

> Do not be afraid of those who kill the body but cannot kill the soul. Rather, be afraid of the One [God] who can destroy both soul and body in hell. (Matthew 10:28)

So how is the fear of the Lord different from situational fear or generalized anxiety? Those can actually intersect if we are thinking of God as a judgmental deity focused primarily on handing out punishment. But in the Bible fear of the Lord [God] actually references having a deep awe and holy reverence for God and submission of our own will to God. It is a recognition that God is all-powerful, all-sovereign, and all-knowing. Since he alone has ultimate control over our lives and destiny, if we fear God (reverence/awe) and submit to his authority, we don't need to fear anything else.

One analogy that can help us understand this is the difference between the servile fear of a slave towards an oppressive master who might lash out with a whip if the slave fails to satisfy and the healthy respect of a child towards a loving but firm parent. The child wants to please the parent and knows that disobedience or rebellion can bring unpleasant consequences. But the child also has complete assurance of the parent's love and their own position as son or daughter. The child also knows—or comes to know—that discipline resulting from disobedience/rebellion is applied with loving intent to help the child become a mature adult (Hebrews 12:5-6).

Unlike other fear, appropriate fear of the Lord has a positive effect on our lives and character. There is a reason describing someone as a

"God-fearing" person is a compliment. Just take a look at a few of the fruits of godly fear mentioned in the book of Proverbs.

The fear of the LORD is the beginning of knowledge, but fools despise wisdom and instruction. (Proverbs 1:7)

The fear of the LORD is to hate evil; pride and arrogance and the evil way and the perverse mouth I hate. (Proverbs 8:13)

The fear of the LORD is the beginning of wisdom, and knowledge of the Holy One is understanding. (Proverbs 9:10)

The fear of the LORD is a fountain of life, that one may avoid the snares of death. (Proverbs 14:27)

The fear of the LORD leads to life so that one may sleep satisfied, untouched by evil. (Proverbs 19:33)

An appropriate fear of our almighty Creator leads us to wisdom, knowledge, and life while leading us away from evil, pride, arrogance, and other sin. Conversely, when people don't appropriately fear God, they figure no one will hold them accountable and that they can do whatever evil they can get away with (Psalm 36:1, Romans 3:18). God will indeed judge those who refuse to fear him just as he poured out judgment on the Israelites for continual disobedience (Isaiah 26:21, Zephaniah 1:2, Romans 2:5-6).

The good news is that those who fear God don't have to live with continued dread of God's punishment for sin and wrong-doing because God sent the ultimate sacrifice to ensure our right-standing with himself through his only Son, Jesus Christ.

> For he [God] made him [Jesus] who knew no sin to
> be sin for us, that we might become the righteousness
> of God in him. (2 Corinthians 5:21)

Jesus became our sin and received all punishment for all our sins—past, present, and future—into his body. So if we've placed our faith in Jesus Christ, then we've been cleansed of all sins we have ever committed or will commit. All consequences of sin, including guilt, shame, condemnation, oppression, depression, fear, disease, and disorder, have been paid in full in the body of Christ Jesus. And our record of debt that the enemy could have held against us has been destroyed and put away forever!

> And we, who were dead in our trespasses and the
> uncircumcision of your flesh, God made alive
> together with him, having forgiven us all our
> trespasses, by canceling the record of debt that
> stood against us with its legal demands. This he
> set aside, nailing it to the cross. He disarmed the
> rulers and authorities and put them to open shame,
> by triumphing over them (once and for all) in him.
> (Colossians 2:12-15)

In the book of Acts, the early church experienced the fear of the Lord when miracles, signs, and wonders took place (Acts 1:43; 3:9-10; 5:5,11). This fear drew all those who witnessed these events to Jesus and to the God who caused the sick to be healed, the lame to walk, and other languages to be spoken by the power of the Holy Spirit.

So we can see that reverential fear of the Lord draws us to him. It is beneficial in fostering a healthy respect for Father God's authority as well as a desire to honor and obey our heavenly Father, his holy Word, and his plans and purposes for our lives.

ACTIVITY D: Who Is Your Daddy?

The concept of an unconditionally loving, adoring heavenly Father was inconceivable for me because it was not demonstrated at home. Maybe you can identify with that. What was your relationship with your father? Non-existent? Abusive? Conditionally loving? Affirmation withheld? Manipulative, demanding, abusive, unstable? Or was it pretty good. Or maybe even really, really good? Take a moment and describe it.

_____

_____

_____

_____

_____

_____

_____

_____

_____

_____

_____

CHAPTER FIVE

PRICE OF PEACE

*"The punishment that brought us peace was on
him, and by his wounds we are healed."*

ISAIAH 53:5

As I learned the hard way, fear is learned. Fear is inherited. Fear is a weapon. Fear is a spirit. Fear is the devil's death trap. Eradicating fear is critical to living the "life more abundantly" that Jesus promises. But how can we achieve that? What does the absence of fear even look like?

When I try to sum up just what an absence of fear looks like in my life, I come back to one single word that best encapsulates this. Peace. Can you visualize what that feels like? That untroubled, calm, serene, relaxed, safe feeling that encompasses all the people around you without a drop of anxiety or fear or anger or hatred.

Maybe you've lived with fear so long that you can't even imagine any more what peace feels like. If you were to do a litmus test, what would your state-of-peace results be? Here are some images to visualize that might help you evaluate.

- Am I swimming with all my might just to stay afloat in dark, raging seas? That's FEAR!
- Am I floating in a placid lake on a chaise-lounge, basking in the warmth of the Son? Sure, I see a storm all around me, but it can't overturn me. That's PEACE!
- Am I backstroking through a sea of regret? That's FEAR!
- Am I snorkeling through crystal-clear water, enjoying the colorful beauty of God's creation all around me? Sure, I see sharks, but they can't eat me. That's PEACE!

There's no pretending that a state of peace is just a day at the beach. But it is attainable to each and every one of us. In fact, it is our birth right. It is God's plan for us. It is our inheritance.

But peace is also a choice. And until we make that choice, nothing else I can share of my journey and in this book will make a difference in banishing fear. Peace comes from choosing the only Person who can give us peace—Jesus Christ. Jesus promises to all who will receive it:

> Peace I leave with you; my peace I give you. I do not
> give to you as the world gives. Do not let your hearts
> be troubled and do not be afraid. (John 14:27)

His Chastisement in Exchange for Our Peace

But that peace comes at a price. A price to Jesus, the sinless Son of God who took upon himself our sins and hurts and fears when he died on the cross in our place. When the prophet Isaiah foresaw the coming of the Savior, he spoke of Jesus taking on the punishment, or chastisement, for our transgressions, our iniquities, so that we in return might have peace and be healed.

> But He was wounded for our transgressions, He was
> bruised for our iniquities; the chastisement for our
> **peace** was upon Him, and by His stripes we are
> **healed**. (Isaiah 53:5, NKJV)

Now let me make clear here that this was no easy, inexpensive, bargain-basement gift. The price Jesus paid for our peace was yanked piece by bloody piece—flesh, muscle, and sinew slashed, and shredded—from our Savior's back. I don't think we the church as the body of Christ teach the crucifixion of Christ in literal, explicit detail often enough. In fact, I think we undervalue the payment Jesus made for us. If you've ever seen the movie *The Passion of the*

Christ, you will have some idea of the excruciating, dehumanizing, gruesome cost of the stripes Jesus endured on our behalf even before he went to the cross.

So how do we receive that gift of peace and healing for which Jesus paid such a high price? By placing our faith in Jesus Christ and freely receiving his gift of salvation.

> Therefore, since we have been justified through faith, we have peace with God through our Lord Jesus Christ. (Romans 5:1)

> For the wages of sin is death, but the gift of God is eternal life in Christ Jesus our Lord. (Romans 6:23)

> If you confess with your mouth the Lord Jesus and believe in your heart that God has raised Him from the dead, you will be saved. (Romans 10:9)

Nor did our Lord and Savior die a criminal's death just so we could have eternal life with him in heaven, glorious as that alone is. The price he paid was vastly more costly and extensively more valuable than that. Notice the pronoun "our" in the above verse. *Our* transgressions. *Our* iniquities. *Our* chastisement.

Jesus was tortured, brutalized, and died in ghastly, humiliating, and excruciatingly painful ways so that we could walk straight out of the consequences of our sins—past, present, and future. He took on himself not only our sin and shortcomings but also the consequences of our sin so that we walk straight into freedom with head held high, unfettered, detangled from pain, emotional trauma, sickness, fear, and dread. Not someday in heaven. Here! Now! Forever! That's the life more abundantly that Jesus promises.

He fully paid the price for righting our wrongs, placing us forever in right standing with our Father (righteousness). He also paid the price for our peace, for our emotional and physical health. And Jesus was not the only One who paid the price. All of heaven paid a weighty price for losing Jesus for a time. Above all, his heavenly Father, *our* heavenly Father, paid a heartbreaking price to witness the betrayal, rejection, and savage abuse of his one and only Son.

But like God the Son, God the Father was willing to pay that price because of his infinite, compassionate love for his sinful, broken, frightened creation. God did not want to abandon us to the consequences of our sinfulness as we are reminded in what is perhaps the best-known Bible verse in the world.

> For **God so loved the world that He gave His only begotten Son**, that whoever believes in Him should not perish but have everlasting life. (John 3:16)

Isn't that a wonderful thought? We are treasured, valued, and deeply loved by the Creator of All. It is an injustice to our Creator and our Savior not to gladly accept our healing and peace for which he has paid the price. Are you ready to receive the peace, identity, and purpose Jesus died to give you? I hope and pray so because only in so doing can you go on to find the healing and freedom from fear we will be learning about in the rest of this book.

CHAPTER SIX

HEALING MIRACLE

"See, I have engraved you on the palms of my hands."

ISAIAH 49:16

Thankfully, even in the midst of a fear-filled childhood, I had a very tender relationship with Jesus. This was due in great measure to my momma, who spent many hours teaching her five children about a loving Savior, instilling God's Word into our hearts and lives, and praying with us.

Among the verses Momma taught me was the verse heading this chapter—Isaiah 49:16. Over and over, she would tell me that God was always thinking of me. That he had great plans for my life. That he loved me so much he had my very name imprinted on the palms of his hands.

Because of Momma's teaching, I knew Jesus didn't bring harm or fear. That was Satan's job. Yes, Jesus loves me, as goes the gospel chorus we sang as children. In fact, he surely loved me since he miraculously healed me of a bone tumor when I was ten years old.

We were still living in our Arkansas home by the chicken factory when I began experiencing terrible pain in my left arm. By the time we moved to the larger town, the symptoms were full-blown and agonizing, especially when I experienced sudden cooler temperatures such as getting out of a bath or walking through the dairy aisle of a grocery store. I carried a jacket with me even in summer. My family prayed for my arm. Our church prayed for my arm.

When my left arm became noticeably smaller than the right from lack of use, I was finally taken to see a bone specialist. After examining my X-rays, the doctor consulted with Momma, using terminology like biopsy and malignancy. On the ride home, Momma was tight-lipped and solemn. When I asked her to explain what the doctor had said, she only responded, "Honey, we need Jesus to heal your arm."

While I didn't really understand everything the doctor had said, I grasped that a biopsy meant going into my arm to get a piece of the tumor. It sounded terrifying and painful, and I definitely didn't want that.

In the end, I didn't have to worry because we never went back to the bone specialist or any other doctor on the matter. With our family of seven, we couldn't afford health insurance, and in any case my father would have considered having it a lack of faith. He also had a strong distrust of doctors and the medical industry, believing them to be crooks just out to make money. Annual physicals were given at the school for participation in P.E. and sports, so visits to the family doctor were only for major emergencies. I saw our family doctor at most five times in my life.

My arm apparently didn't amount to a major emergency, so my parents settled into a wait-and-see approach, though I'm sure if I'd taken a serious turn for the worse, they'd have permitted medical intervention. For my part, I had no doubt that Jesus could heal me. Momma and I began reading together and memorizing Scripture verses on healing. One in particular resonated with me:

Who Himself bore our sins in His own body on the tree, that we, having died to sins, might live for righteousness—by whose stripes you were healed. (1 Peter 2:24, Berean Study Bible)

The verse was actually quoting from Isaiah 53:5, the verse we looked at in the last chapter, which speaks of the healing we receive through the "stripes" or suffering Jesus endured when he died for us on the cross. The original passage reads, "By his stripes we *are* healed." But when the apostle Peter referred to that passage in his epistle, he used the past tense: "you *were* healed."

I remember vividly when the significance of this struck me. I was getting into the bathtub, already dreading getting back out and drying off because that part was so painful.

"By whose stripes you were healed," I recited to myself as I slid down into the warm water. "By whose stripes you were healed. Wait, you *were* healed? That means I'm ALREADY healed! Momma, come quick!"

Momma came running in. She looked worried, but her concern melted away when she saw my excited face. "What it is, honey?"

"I'm healed! I'm healed!" I exclaimed.

"How do you know?" Momma asked excitedly. "Does it feel any different?"

"No, not yet." I went on to explain how the difference between Isaiah 53:5 and 1 Peter 2:24 proved I was already healed. Momma's face fell a bit, but she tried not to look disappointed that my healing hadn't yet manifested itself.

By His Stripes

Let's take a minute to focus on the "stripes" mentioned in Isaiah 53:5 and 1 Peter 2:24. The Hebrew word used in Isaiah is the Hebrew word *chaburah*, which is actually a singular word meaning a black and blue mark. The image is not of individual weal of lacerated skin, but one continuous, open black-and-blue wound or bruise. In other words, not a shred of skin was left on our Savior's back. Jesus endured that level of extreme pain so that we might be granted healing. That is love!

There is a divine exchange that takes place in healing, whether physical or emotional. We bring our pain, trauma, injury, and suffering and exchange it for the healing and wholeness purchased by our almighty Jesus. It seems so incomprehensibly unfair that a sinless, perfect Savior should have to take on all our "gunk." But that is grace. Grace is for the undeserving. That's me. That's you. Our Father God planned this amazing grace for us from before the foundation of the world.

And whether physical or emotional, the healing work is already completed. As he hung from the cross, Jesus proclaimed, "It is finished (John 19:30)!" This means he had fully completed the work of our redemption and restoration. The finished work of the cross ensures we are forevermore holy, restored, righteous, redeemed, and healed from every dis-ease, dis-comfort, dis-order and un-rest.

Interestingly, any word starting with the prefixes "dis" or "un" signals that the word's meaning is the exact opposite, or complete lack of, its root word. So dis-ease, dis-comfort, and dis-order reference a complete lack of ease, comfort, or order while un-rest, un-loved, un-happy, un-kind describes a complete lack of rest, love, happiness, kindness. Our Savior's stripes have purchased for us healing from these prefixes. Instead of dis-ease, dis-comfort, dis-order, un-rest, un-loved, un-kindness, and so many more un-happy words, Jesus offers ease, comfort, order, rest, love, kindness, along with righteousness, peace, and joy.

When we aren't walking in this truth, it's because we are carrying a false I.D. card in our wallet. Our identity might have our picture on it, but the details are all wrong because we do not understand our value, our worth, and how much we are treasured and loved.

Back then at the age of ten, I didn't know much about divine healing, and I certainly didn't understand all the spiritual implications those passages held. But I was certain this was a revelation from Jesus. I grabbed onto that revelation and clung to it, repeating it out loud many times a day every time the enemy reminded me of pain in my body. And ultimately I received the healing Jesus paid for me. I can't explain it any other way.

It took about a year for healing to become evident. But no matter how my arm felt, I was resolute that I'd been healed. Momma finally took me to the family doctor for an X-ray, which confirmed the miracle. The doctor was absolutely speechless at my healthy, unscarred bone and the total absence of any tumor.

Activity E: Tracing Fear to Its Source

We've talked about our fears, whether learned or inherited. We've also recognized that these fears do not come from God. Now let's see if we can trace our various traumas and inherited fears to the resulting fear-based behaviors. Write your learned/inherited fears from Activity A and B in the first column and your fear behaviors from Activity C in the second column. Draw a line from each fear inducer to its resulting behavior.

These connections could be one-to-one but are often one-to-many and many-to-one. Meaning that one trauma or inheritance could result in multiple fear behaviors. Not all fear behaviors are readily traceable to a specific trauma or inherited fear, but as you pray, the Holy Spirit will reveal them to you. Again, if you need more room, do this exercise in your journal.

Learned/Inherited Fears
(from Activity A and B)

Fear-Based Behaviors
from Activity C above)

_____

_____

_____

_____

_____

_____

_____

CHAPTER SEVEN

COPING

"And surely I am with you always, to the very end of the age."
MATTHEW 28:20

You might be hoping that accepting our Lord and Savior's gift of salvation and eternal life would be enough to permanently banish that spirit of fear so we can live the rest of our lives in peace, joy, and the fullness of our God-ordained potential. Sadly, that isn't always or even usually the case. Remember that peace is a choice. And banishing the spirit of fear is an ongoing battle.

Later on we are going to walk through the battle plan for banishing fear and conquering negative strongholds that God revealed to me in my darkness. But to experience Holy Spirit-bestowed strength and dynamite power (*dunamis*), there are some questions we need to answer and truths we need to know about ourselves.

Who are we?

Why were we created?

What is God's original and ongoing plan for our lives?

In other words, we need to understand our identity, our purpose, and our inheritance as a child of God. Why is this so important? I mentioned earlier that our enemy is a thief and a liar whose goal is to steal our identity as God's child. Fear is Satan's chief contaminating weapon he uses to poison our peace and joy. Few of us are unscathed by its toxic touch.

Conversely, understanding who, what, why, and above all, Whose we are is our first defensive weapon against the enemy's fear attacks. The long-term trauma, injury, and hurts we've endured are exacerbated by aligning ourselves with an inaccurate identity. You see, like peace, what we choose to believe and claim as our identity is a choice. And if what we believe and claim as our identity doesn't align with what Jesus died to give us, it's the wrong one!

In fact, the battles against the enemy are won or lost right here before we even get in on the fight. Why? Because we must grasp that what we pray and ask for we will receive. Not because of who we are or what we do, but because of Whose we are, what he's already done, and what he will continue to do to assure us the victory.

That was certainly the case with me. While I knew Jesus loved me, I couldn't reconcile Jesus with the terror that reigned in our home. Nor could I conceive of myself as an adored, protected daughter of a loving heavenly Father any more than I could conceive of being loved by my own father or safe in my own home.

As I reached adolescence, I realized I was capable of figuring out coping mechanisms to navigate my dangerous environment as well as setting goals to escape. This included keeping myself busy and away from home. I began applying myself at school, in athletics, and with part-time jobs.

I also sought a remedy for the pain and sadness of my relationship with my father by filling life with activities and friends so that I could experience fun and laughter as well as avoid being home. I had my first steady boyfriend at age fifteen and was involved in my first serious relationship at sixteen. I excelled in school and did well in athletics and work. My goal was to become independent and financially stable as quickly as possible, and I was willing to work night and day to ensure that happened.

I did just that. After high school, I attended Hendrix College, an academically strenuous private college about an hour's drive from my home. My family couldn't help pay for college, which meant working thirty hours per week to pay what loans and grants didn't cover.

It also meant spending more time away from Momma, whom I loved more than anyone or anything else in my life. I knew she was very unhappy, especially now that the last of her children had left home, and I wanted desperately to give her a better, happier life than she'd had with my father. I was driven to succeed academically in part so I could have a successful career that would ensure a better future for Momma as well as myself. At the same time, I was afraid I'd fail in that mission. I worried constantly that Momma would die before I got the chance.

That goal and focus became a large portion of my identity. I graduated from Hendrix College with a Bachelor of Arts in Psychology. After a semester off, I enrolled at the University of Arkansas at Little Rock, graduating in eighteen months with a Master of Applied Psychology. I felt well on my way to a career in corporate management.

But though outwardly I appeared outgoing, happy, and fun, in reality I was deeply insecure and constantly afraid of being incorrect, rejected, embarrassed, or shamed. I vacillated between defiant independence and insecurity. I hated being alone and craved affirmation like an addict while insisting on being in control.

One thing I swore was that I would never permit my fate to lie in the hands of a man. I'd determined this from witnessing the feelings of failure and disappointment Momma faced day in and day out. She retained a great deal of guilt for the painful childhood her children had endured and for not standing up against the horrific disciplinary measures Dad employed. She'd been there to hear our desperate pleas for mercy and prolonged screaming.

In part, Momma's feeling of guilt and powerlessness stemmed from her own childhood when she and her siblings had lived in terror of their oldest brother as he preyed upon them, stalked them, and physically abused them. The worst was that she could do nothing to prevent him from repeatedly molesting her five-year-old baby sister. Now she'd ended up in a marriage where she could do nothing to protect her own children from their abuser. Or so she felt.

Meanwhile, my own heart had become a revolving door where boyfriend after boyfriend waltzed in and out, each taking a piece of my heart and self-worth, further eroding my fragile faith that God esteemed me important. I was unable to say no to men or to anyone in authority. I stopped attending church once I started college, and the "way of the world" became my new normal, including alcohol, smoking, partying, and unwholesome relationships with the opposite gender.

I dated one man several years older than me for four years, my longest relationship to date. Though I had hopes of a future, including marriage and children with this man, the relationship devolved into great dysfunction wrought with disloyalty, jealousy and distrust.

I realized I needed to put major distance between myself and him. An opportunity came up for a position that was vaguely in my field of corporate management. It wasn't a high-level or well-paying job, just a general staffing position in a software company. But it was in Florida, many hundreds of miles from my ex-boyfriend. So I took it, and Florida gradually became my home right to the present day.

This was the heyday of businesses shifting to computerized systems, and helping companies with installing software systems and the training to use these systems was a growing industry. I took a new job where my role included learning software systems and database structures so I could in turn teach corporate clients how to use them. I discovered that I excelled at this work and was soon making a good salary. All I'd hoped for when leaving home for college was coming true.

Now I was ready to offer Momma her own new and better future.

CHAPTER EIGHT

TRAUMA OF LOSS

"Hope deferred makes the heart sick, but a dream fulfilled is a tree of life. People who despise advice are asking for trouble; those who respect a command will succeed. The instruction of the wise is like a life-giving fountain; those who accept it avoid the snares of death."

I had been in Florida a couple years when I learned that Momma had lung cancer. With no health insurance and Dad's mindset against doctors, they'd adopted the same pray, have faith, and wait-and-see approach when Momma began feeling symptoms as with my bone tumor. Only months later when the pain was so bad she could hardly walk did they finally seek medical treatment. By that point, the cancer had spread throughout her body and into her bones.

I prayed passionately for her healing. After all, hadn't Jesus healed my childhood tumor? In my earlier years, Momma had prophesied repeatedly that God had great plans for my life and would use me in mighty ways, including spreading the gospel of Jesus and miraculous healing. I can remember as young as five years old how Momma would hold my small hands and say to me, "These little hands will do great things. Your name Ami means beloved, set apart, consecrated to God, and you are destined for greatness. The least will become the first."

Years later when I was fourteen, I attended a tent revival with Momma. One of the evangelists speaking at the conference came over to Momma and me and prayed for us. He also prophesied over me, saying to both of us that my hands held the gift of divine healing. Momma just about burst with maternal pride to hear this man of God confirm what she had been praying and prophesying over me since my earliest childhood.

FEAR NOT! UNLEASH THE CONQUEROR WITHIN

Now a dozen years after that revival, I wasn't following God or even attending church. But from the moment I learned she was sick, I prayed desperately for my momma. Up to that point, I'd made the trip home for major holidays every few months. Now I took an hourly consulting job so I could be with Momma for each chemotherapy treatment. I missed her fourth treatment, needing to work to pay for my next flight home, but was with her for her final treatment.

She was so happy to leave the hospital and chemo behind that she felt she was being sprung out of jail. We were both confident God would heal her, but the disease was aggressive, and despite our prayers and desperation, she wasted away in front of us. I made a trip to Florida to work for four weeks. By the time I returned, she couldn't hide the gravity of her condition and I couldn't hide my sorrow. We held each other and cried. She died just two weeks afterward. She was only fifty-six. I knew she was now with her Savior Jesus Christ, but my heart felt shattered, my spirit broken. How could God have placed the gift of healing in my hands when all my fervent prayers hadn't even affected healing for my own precious momma?

"God must not mean anything he said about me, Momma, or anything else!" my mind cried out. "Either God's Word is dead, or he's a liar!"

With my momma's death, all my dreams of making a better life for her evaporated and with them the basis for my identity. Gone was any remaining faith that God cared for me. Yes, Jesus loved me, but Sovereign God certainly did not. For the next decade, I struggled with an identity crisis, living a worldly, scandalous lifestyle, allowing the trauma of loss and pain to block out any light of truth. God was still speaking to me, but I didn't want to listen so I just gave him the "talk to the hand" signal.

Out of pain and disappointment, I'd curated my own theology that God favors only those who live very righteously. That certainly was not me! I could never do enough to please him, so I figured I might as well wash my hands of the whole religion thing and be done with trying to live righteously.

Instead, I focused on my career, establishing myself in the

software industry as a well-respected implementation consultant, software trainer, business analyst, and product manager. I excelled at my job and was very proud of that. In fact, I couldn't imagine ever not working.

"I've worked too hard to get here!" I told myself. "I'll never NOT work."

By this point, my siblings were all married and busy raising their own families. Dad started attending a new church and became very involved with it. He did make time for me during the years of grieving. We even took a couple of vacations together.

I met Scott in 2002 at a software company where we were both tenured. Originally from Long Island, New York, he too had transplanted to Florida. After a few different jobs, he found a role within the same software company. Also an implementation consultant and the best mentor of the entire consulting department, he was sought after by colleagues and customers alike for his technical knowledge, problem solving, and expert crisis diffusion capabilities.

As part of the implementation department, Scott and I traveled all over the U.S., occasionally working on the same projects and even traveling together. At this time he was married to his first wife. I found out later that Scott found me attractive, but he never flirted in any way, not even with his eyes. I really respected him for that.

Scott's marriage eventually ended in divorce. We began dating not quite a year later. By this time I'd grown tired of the suitcase life, so I'd shifted to a position in product management that offered good pay, seniority, and an excellent title without all the travel.

We enjoyed a whirlwind romance and found so many things about each other that seemed missing from our individual lives: security, belonging, admiration, adoration, and trust. Scott proposed to me after four and a half months of dating, and we were married five months after that in May of 2006. It was a gorgeous family wedding and the kind of honeymoon you dream about. Our first nine months of marriage were romantic and exciting. Scott still traveled frequently for work, and there was still an aroma of freshness in our relationship.

Fast forward through several years of marriage to two little babies of our own. Identity at last! I was a mom as well as a career woman. Purpose—check! Value and meaning—check, check! Successful career that was also an escape route in case our marriage didn't work out—DOUBLE CHECK!! I was queen of my kingdom at last! The Kingdom of Ami!

ACTIVITY F: Created with a Purpose

Do you believe God created you with a purpose for your life? Or maybe you think that's just a fairy tale for dreamers and the very naïve. If the latter, then I'm so glad I've got this time with you! Let me ask you a couple questions. Hint: some of the clues to these questions lie in your strengths, gifts, and talents.

Why do you think you exist?

_____

_____

_____

_____

_____

_____

What do you think is God's purpose for your life?

_____

_____

_____

_____

_____

CHAPTER NINE

IDENTITY

*"I give them eternal life, and they will never perish, and
no one will snatch them out of my hand. My Father, who
has given them to me, is greater than all, and no one
is able to snatch them out of the Father's hand."*

JOHN 10:28-29 (ESV)

Of course in truth, my identity was as false as my kingdom was based on sand, as I would only too quickly find out. Unfortunately, Scott and I both came into our marriage with emotional baggage packed to the brim and spilling over. Left unattended, that baggage was a recipe for disaster.

The first onslaught on our unstable sandy foundation came in February 2007. Scott was an only child of a single mother. His biological father had abandoned them around Scott's first birthday and to this day has never bothered reconnecting with his son. At the age of four, Scott was sexually molested by one of his mother's boyfriends. Both of these traumas added to the internal baggage he was carrying.

Scott's mom had been battling cancer for ten years, and now just nine months after our wedding she became critically ill. Since I'd lost my own momma to this horrible disease, I recognized the familiar signs of death. If we were to spend any significant time with Scott's mom before she died, we needed to relocate quickly.

"You'll never forgive yourself if you aren't there for whatever time she has left," I told Scott, my own pain over being so far away when Momma was diagnosed still sharp in my mind and heart. We both talked to our employers. Since Scott worked with implementation of software projects all over the country, he could live anywhere with easy access to an airport. My own employer informed me, "You can't

42

work as our product manager from NYC. But we can shift you into a business analyst position that will let you work via computer from home."

That settled, Scott and I had our Florida condo packed up within two weeks and moved to a rented home close to where Scott's grandma and relatives lived on Long Island. Scott's mom had been in the hospital due to a recent fall where she'd broken her pelvis. Because of the fall, no further radiation or chemo could be administered to slow down the disease. So she was released into hospice care.

Instead of sending her to a separate facility for care, Scott and I insisted she come live with us. Because of the experience I'd had with Momma, I was confident that with the help of a visiting hospice nurse we could care for her and that she would be most comfortable spending her remaining days surrounded by loved ones and normal family activity. And she was. She passed away just over three weeks after our move. She was sixty-two years young. Now Scott and I both had no mother and felt completely orphaned.

Scott internalized his loss, grieving silently and privately. I thought I was being understanding by giving him space and not pushing him to open up. Scott wasn't much of a talker unless he was drinking, something we both did a lot of. Even then we avoided the topic of his loss. The joy, intimacy, and tenderness of being newly married was replaced by a narrow but deep chasm between us. We never recovered that ground, and I increasingly felt that my precious new identity as loved, valued queen of my own perfect, safe little kingdom was slipping away like the sand it had been built on being washed into the ocean by a storm.

Understand Your Identity

So what does identity even mean? Typically when we want to get to know someone, we find out their name, then go on to ask, "What do you do?" Somehow, we wrap identity into what a person produces. But what we do doesn't define who we are. Think about it. What are all the things you do? For me, I parent, educate, write, help run a business and talk a whole lot! The list goes on and on. But those are things I *do*, not who I *am*. Our true identity lies in our genealogy and purpose for existence. And that takes us back to the very beginning. Back to the very first man and woman—and the very first Father.

Who's Your Daddy?

The book of Genesis tells us how God created the heavens and the earth by simply speaking it into existence. Then God said, "Let us make mankind in our image" (Genesis 1:26-27). The Triune God—Father, Son, and Holy Spirit—had already enjoyed an eternity together. Now Abba Father wanted sons and daughters. So he created Adam and Eve and gave them an intimate, face-to-face relationship with him. As their inheritance, God gave Adam and Eve dominion over all things on earth and created a special home for them in a beautiful garden. As the very first Father, God came regularly to the garden to walk with Adam and Eve in the cool of the day (Genesis 3:8). You can bet they could hardly wait for their daddy's visits.

You probably know what happened next. Adam and Eve disobeyed and totally wrecked their intimate relationship with Father God (Genesis 3). Condemnation, another form of fear, entered the scene. Because of their shame and fear, Adam and Eve hid from God. To protect them from living forever in their sin, God sent them away from the Tree of Life, expelling them from the garden.

The Bible never says that God removed himself from Adam and Eve or stripped them of the power and dominion over all things he'd given them. But in their guilt, condemnation, and fear, they stopped believing in who God had created them to be. Instead of living with an expectation of dominion over all things, they lived in fear of a now-unfriendly, dangerous world. They stopped looking for the Father's presence. They forgot their true identity as did their descendants right down to you and me.

But God did not forget them—or us. God met Adam and Eve

where they were and gave them the promise of a Savior (Genesis 3:15). Down through the ages, we see God reaffirming his covenant with Noah, Abraham, Moses, and the Israelites to redeem and restore what was lost in the Garden of Eden. A redemption and restoration that was accomplished through the sacrifice and resurrection of God's one and only Son, Jesus.

That's why Jesus is called our Redeemer because he has restored us to a right standing, or a right relationship, with our Creator. And not just any relationship. Scripture tells us that when we place our faith in Jesus we are adopted as sons (and daughters) into God's family. In fact, before the creation of the world, before Adam and Eve ever sinned, God already knew we would need redemption and had already made plans to provide for our adoption through the finished work of Christ on the cross.

> For he chose us in him before the creation of the world to be holy and blameless in his sight. In love he predestined us for adoption to sonship through Jesus Christ, in accordance with his pleasure and will. (Ephesians 1:4-5)

Adoption into Sonship

So, if we've been adopted to sonship, what exactly is our relationship with God? I can answer that because I've recently been through the adoption process (more about that later!). In the eyes of the law, an adoptive son or daughter is every bit as much the child of the adoptive parents as a biological child. And the adoptive parents are every bit as much the mother and father of that child as though they shared the same DNA.

Which means that our Creator God who knew us and planned for adoption before the creation of the world is our heavenly Daddy, our Papa, our Abba. If you've only known an unkind, unloving, harsh earthly father or even one who is simply absent or indifferent, that might not trigger happy thoughts, in fact maybe even frightening ones. Thankfully, the Bible shows us a very different image. Look at some of the character traits Scripture describes of our heavenly Father.

> The Lord is **gracious** and **full of compassion, slow to anger** and **great in mercy**. The Lord is **good to all**, and His **tender mercies** are over all His works. (Psalms 145:8-9, NKJV)

> The Lord, the **compassionate** and **gracious** God, **slow to anger, abounding in love** and **faithfulness**, maintaining love to thousands, and **forgiving** wickedness, rebellion and sin. (Exodus 34:6-7)

> Who is a God like you, who **pardons sin** and **forgives** the transgression of the remnant of his inheritance? You **do not stay angry** forever but **delight to show mercy**. You will again have **compassion** on us; you will tread our sins underfoot and hurl all our iniquities into the depths of the sea. (Micah 7:18-19)

> Now return to the LORD your God, For he is **gracious** and **compassionate, slow to anger**, abounding in **lovingkindness** and relenting of evil. (Joel 2:13, NASB)

> Therefore the LORD longs to be **gracious** to you, And therefore he waits on high to have **compassion** on you For the LORD is a God of **justice**; How blessed are all those who long for Him. (Isaiah 30:18, NASB)

> Just as a father has compassion on his children, So the LORD has **compassion** on those who fear him.

> For he himself knows our frame; he is mindful that
> we are but dust. (Psalms 103:13-14, NASB)

> Know therefore that the Lord your God is God; he
> is the **faithful** God, **keeping his covenant of love to
> a thousand generations** of those who love him and
> keep his commandments. (Deuteronomy 7:9)

> But from **everlasting to everlasting** the **LORD's love**
> is with those who fear him, and his **righteousness**
> with their children's children. (Psalm 103:17)

Wow, that is the kind of father we all long for! Our heavenly Daddy isn't angry with us or looking for opportunities to punish us for every small infraction—or even large ones. He is compassionate, gracious, merciful, forgiving, loving, faithful. He is slow to anger, a characteristic that means a lot to me. In other words, he doesn't have a hair-trigger temper but is patient and even-tempered even when his children make mistakes. Nor is he loving, compassionate, merciful, and forgiving for just a short while until he gets tired of our failures, but to a thousand generations. No, more than that. From everlasting to everlasting.

God is sovereign, all-knowing, all-powerful, and all providing. He gives good and perfect gifts (James 1:17). Papa God also grieves with us when we grieve. He hears those who are brokenhearted and crushed in spirit (Psalms 34:17-18). He catches and records every tear we shed (Psalms 56:8). But he doesn't stop there. He personally rescues us, lifts us up, and even carries us in times of hardship and pain.

> In all their suffering He [God] also suffered, and He
> personally rescued them. In His love and mercy, He
> redeemed them. He lifted them up and carried them
> through all the years. (Isaiah 63:9, NLT)

47

And check this out! When we are knocked down, our heavenly Daddy sings songs of deliverance over us! Now, that is a tender-hearted Papa!

> You are my hiding place; you will protect me from trouble and surround me with songs of deliverance. (Psalms 32:7)

God Is Love

But the most wonderful, important characteristic of our heavenly Father isn't just what He is like but who He is. The Bible tells us that God isn't just loving. God *is* love.

> Whoever does not love does not know God, because **God is love**. This is how **God's love** was revealed among us: God sent His one and only Son into the world, so that we might live through Him. And love consists in this: not that we loved God, but that **He loved us** and sent His Son as an atoning sacrifice for our sins . . . **God is love**; whoever abides in love abides in God, and God in him. (1 John 4:8-10, 16)

That is a lot of mention of love. In fact, there are many further mentions in the entire passage, if you'd like to check that out (1 John 4:7-21). But what this passage is telling us is that God demonstrates loving characteristics toward us and does loving things for us (like sending his Son to atone for our sins) because he can do nothing else. God *is* love, so every thought, emotion, and action of God must be born of who he is—love!

Why is that so important to a discussion on fear and how to banish fear from our lives? The answer is in the very next verses of that passage.

> There is no fear in love, but perfect love drives out
> fear, because fear involves punishment. The one
> who fears has not been perfected in love. We love
> because he first loved us. (1 John 4:18-19)

What does this mean for you and me? Simply put, since God is Love, then fear doesn't come from God. Since God's very essence is Love and he created you and me in his image, he created us to love and be loved by him. He didn't create us to be governed by fear or any of its many flavors, including anxiety, oppression, compulsive disorders, depression.

We are afraid of a harsh, angry earthly father because we know that punishment is right around the corner just waiting for our next slip-up to pounce. But there is no anger in God toward us—only love. We don't need to live in constant fear that our heavenly Father is looking for opportunities to punish us. Far from it, he is looking for opportunities to bless us, prosper us, and shower us in his mercy, loving kindness, favor, and success!

Which brings us back to our original question and the reason for writing this book. How do we banish the spirit of fear from our lives? Love. God. God *is* love. So as we let God's love into our lives, as we are perfected in his love—i.e., let God's love control us more and more—then that spirit of fear simply can't stick around anymore because our enemy can't co-exist with God/Love any more than a snowman can co-exist with a bonfire.

Later on, we'll get specific on just how we can allow God's love to perfect us and drive out fear. But for now I hope you have a clear understanding of your true identity as a loved child of a loving heavenly Daddy. That is, if you have accepted God's gift of adoption into his family through the atoning sacrifice of Jesus Christ (1 John 4:10). If you haven't, please don't waste any more time in accepting his wonderful gift.

ACTIVITY G: A Portrait of Our Heavenly Daddy

The verses I've quoted in the prior chapter are only a sample of what the Bible has to say about our heavenly Father's character. Do a word search on the following terms to see how deep and wide God's character as a compassionate, gracious, merciful, forgiving, faithful, good, and loving heavenly Father is revealed throughout the Bible. List as many scripture passages as you can find.

_____

_____

_____

_____

_____

1 Corinthians 13 is often called the love chapter, especially verses 4-7, which describe the characteristics of love. Since God IS love, read this chapter aloud from your favorite Bible version, replacing the word "love" with God. For example, instead of "love is patient" (vs.), read as "God is patient." How does this description of God/Love change your perception of your heavenly Father? Journal your thoughts on this below.

_____

_____

_____

_____

CHAPTER TEN

PURPOSE

"Where could I go from your Spirit? Where could I run and hide from your face? If I go up to heaven, you're there! If I go down to the realm of the dead, you're there too! Wherever I go, your hand will guide me; your strength will empower me. It's impossible to disappear from you or ask the darkness to hide me, for your presence is everywhere, bringing light into the night."

PSALMS 139:7-8, 10-11, TPT

With the reason for our move to New York now gone, Scott and I weren't sure what to do next. Since our jobs allowed for flexibility of location, we really had no limits as to where we decided to go next so long as there was a reliable airport for Scott and reliable internet for me. Scott leaned toward remaining in New York or moving back to Florida. I had purchased some acreage in Colorado before we began dating, so I leaned toward beginning a new adventure out west.

In the end, we moved to Denver. Our daughter Elsa (named after my mom) was born there in 2010 and our son Gaetano (named after Scott's grandfather), Guy for short, in 2011. Since we both had good-paying jobs, we could afford to hire a nanny to care for our children during those hours I worked from a home office. Scott continued his prior travel at first for the same company he'd worked for in Florida and New York. But he too was tiring of the suitcase life. A devoted father, he wanted to spend more time with his small children.

He eventually shifted within the company to mentoring up-and-coming implementation consultants, which permitted him to drastically cut his traveling. Then a position as director of applications opened up at a Denver college. Once he took that job, neither of us had to travel as much, and could dedicate ourselves to our family. Even grieving the loss of our mothers and a family life virtually devoid of God's presence, life was seeming good.

But with a history of poor or non-existent relationships with our fathers and the trauma of childhood abuse, neither Scott nor I had a successful track record of healthy relationships. The relationships we'd both had before our marriage were built on attraction, if not lust, and few mutual interests. Our own relationship began with compatibility, security, belonging, mutual respect, and attraction but not a solid friendship. And certainly not with the foundation principle of God as the center.

Looking back, I can see that our love for each other depended largely on how we made the other feel at that moment in time. We didn't know how to cultivate intimacy with each other beyond the bedroom or deep trust during hard times, which came more often once we started having children. Despite my own unhealthy relationships before our marriage, I'd been raised in an extremely conservative household, and if Scott so much as noticed an attractive woman walking by, I saw it as complete betrayal. He in turn felt I was totally overreacting.

"I'm a married man," he'd say. "Not a dead one."

Scott and I attended a few marriage counseling sessions. But to me it seemed to me the counselor was always making excuses for Scott. "Well, you see, Ami, Scott's mom died recently, so he feels like his rock, his steadfast center, all that he's known and relied on, has been removed."

"Well, you know what?" I wanted to scream back. "My momma died too! Why am I the bad person here?"

I never felt we came to any resolutions. To me, it felt like Scott wasn't identifying with my hurt or my needs. I'm sure he felt the same. Though we kept moving forward as marriage and parental partners, we'd not only lost our intimacy but didn't even know we should fight for it. I became bitterly disappointed in our marriage. And it showed in my attitude and behavior.

The bigger issue was that the intimacy we craved was much deeper than our physical relationship. Our joint abandonment and abuse histories had left emotional scar tissue so thick we couldn't fully develop deeper levels of a healthy relationship like trust, belonging, safety, hopes, dreams, desires. The chasm in our marriage widened, and once again I found myself doubting the identity I'd worked so hard to establish, whether indeed I had value to anyone besides my children who depended on me, much less the man I loved and thought loved me. Was there actually any purpose to my life beyond simply surviving one more day?

Understand Your Purpose

"Who am I that I even matter? Why do I exist anyway? God, who do YOU say I am?"

Have you ever asked God those questions? I certainly have, especially after hard stops and starts. When I don't feel I'm more than a conqueror because I'm sucking wind from a sucker punch. When I can't rely on those closest to me to help rebuild confidence and hope because it was they who dealt the sucker punch. Can you identify?

After we take a long, hard look at our heavenly Father, we need to understand in our innermost being that there is a plan and purpose for our lives. That our lives have meaning and value. That what we are walking through now is worth enduring. That on the other side of this heartbreak and hardship is a treasure of intimacy and wisdom that makes it all worthwhile. That we aren't just the result of a man and a woman procreating, a mere product of biology.

So why then do I exist? Why do you exist? The short answer is **relationship**. Specifically, a relationship of love. We've already learned that God's most notable characteristic is love. God *is* love. God created us because he wanted to share his great love and his glorious family—Father, Spirit and Son—with his children, all who have believed on the name of Jesus (John 1:12, Ephesians 2:4-5). I believe God replicated this same desire in our DNA. When we marry and plan a family, we do so with the same objective in mind—a relationship of love.

The longer answer is **purpose.** I'm not talking about ordinary human goals like live a good life, be happy, retire in a great community, get married, have a family, become _ (whatever your dream, just fill in the blank), take care of my parents when they are old. All good stuff, but I'm talking about purpose and destiny so awesome and exciting you know it's hand-tailored made to fit you! The kind of stuff that makes you jump up out of bed early in the mornings just because you are so passionate about it.

That's right. God stood at the foundation of creation and thought of me and thought of you. He not only created us in his image to love and be loved by him but to reflect his image, his glory, and his love to others. He designed us and preordained us to bring Kingdom-of-Heaven reality to earth so that his nature and character are in operation here on earth and the whole world can see that truly he is a good, good Father.

We, that's you and me, are created in God's image. He did not create us to be governed by fear or any of its many flavors, including compulsive disorders, depression, oppression, or anxiety. Fear is the domain of the enemy due to his fall from heaven and the fall of man in the Garden of Eden.

We Were Born for Such a Time as This

God also created each of us uniquely. Not only with our own compilation of gifts, strengths, and talents, but at a specific point of human history. Make no mistake. You were created for such a time as this. And because God also created the concept of time, he is not surprised by the latest news and daily reports. He has been in each of our days and knows the challenges we will face, choices we will make, the paths we will take. He has created us and chosen us ON purpose FOR purpose at just the right time. Each of us are essential to God's purpose and plan in this day and age.

But don't take my word for it. Let's take a look at what the basis for all authority, God's Word, says about it.

For you formed my inward parts; you knitted me together in my mother's womb . . . My frame was not hidden from you, when I was being made in secret, intricately woven in the depths of the earth. Your eyes saw my unformed substance; in your book were written, every one of them, the days that were formed for me, when as yet there was none of them. (Psalm 139:13-16, ESV)

Before I formed you [Jeremiah] in the womb, I knew you. Before you were born I sanctified you. I ordained you a prophet to the nations. (Jeremiah 1:5)

For those whom he [God] foreknew he also predestined to be conformed to the image of his Son. (Romans 8:29)

. . . who [God] saved us and called us to a holy calling, not because of our works but because of his own purpose and grace, which he gave us in Christ Jesus before the ages began. (2 Timothy 1:9)

He [God] chose us in him before the foundation of the world, that we should be holy and blameless before him in love, having predestined us to adoption as sons by Jesus Christ to Himself. (Ephesians 1:4-5, ESV)

The glory that you [God] have given me [Jesus] I have given to them that they may be one even as we are one, I in them and you in me, that they may become perfectly one, so that the world may know that you sent me and loved them even as you loved me. (John 17:22-23, ESV)

I cry out to God Most High, to God who fulfills his
purpose for me. (Psalm 57:2, ESV)

In summary, God knit us together in our mother's womb, wrote
down every day of our lives before they happened, chose us before
creation, predestined us to be his children, and called us to be like
Jesus, holy, blameless, united, and loving others the way God loves
us. And God will fulfill his purpose for you. You are unique and
essential to his plan. Great is your value to him!

ACTIVITY H: God, Who Do You Say I Am?

If you haven't already, I encourage you to ask God who he says you are. Ask him what his thoughts were for you when he stood on the foundation of creation. Ask him what the books that have been written about you in heaven have to say. Write down the answers you receive.

_____

_____

_____

_____

_____

Listen when (not if) God begins whispering to you words of value, worth and love. I believe he's already begun. Will you trust him? Commit to paper the affirmations God gives you. Also, consider keeping an ongoing journal of God's communication with you as he speaks in your daytime and in your night-time dreams.

_____

_____

_____

_____

_____

CHAPTER ELEVEN

SPEAK THE WORD

*"Can a mother forget the baby at her breast and
have no compassion on the child she has borne?
Though she may forget, I will not forget you!"*

ISAIAH 49:15

The growing distance between Scott and me was not helped by our second child's almost constant health crises. When we'd decided to have a second baby, we'd prayed for a baby brother for Elsa. We'd planned the timing of his conception and arrival. And our son Gaetano arrived right on time.

But nothing else went as planned. We'd been anticipating a fat, happy ten-pounder just as Scott had been at birth. Instead, Guy was a failure-to-thrive baby, born just five pounds, thirteen ounces. I managed to dehydrate him within his first week, nearly landing him in the hospital. Just keeping him alive and gaining weight was a real challenge. It seemed I was constantly feeding him as he could only take small amounts at a time because it was too tiring for him. He struggled with developmental milestones, missing many by far.

Then just before Guy's second birthday, he began having seizures. The first time this happened was so terrifying and traumatic that Scott and I both thought he was dying. He stopped breathing, turning rigid and blue. I gave him mouth to mouth, and he finally started breathing again. I screamed at Scott to call 911. A harrowing ride in the ambulance landed us in the emergency room. The seizures continued throughout that day and into the night, wracking his tiny, frail body. With each one, I thought he would surely die. Right then and there, I dusted off my prayer language. It had been a while as I hadn't seen much use for it until it was urgently needed. Praying was all I could do for my baby.

Long, horrible story short, baby Guy spent three terrifying nights in the pediatric intensive care unit. He went through intubation and test after test, his tiny head of curls covered in spaghetti wires of probes and electrodes, all hooked up to various monitors. He was finally diagnosed with Influenza A. The spinal tap came back negative while an MRI on his brain showed no sign or cause for epilepsy. All great news! The doctors explained that sometimes small children have seizures with a serious flu virus, and most of them will never have one again.

We hoped and prayed this would be the case with Guy, but it wasn't. Any time he began running a temperature, not even a very high temperature, he'd have a seizure. Where there was one seizure, clusters inevitably followed. Our first child, Elsa, is only seventeen months older than Guy. If you've had small children—or been one—you can envision the constant dirty faces and fingers, boogers, slime, and sneezes. From two to five years of age, Elsa and Guy were often sick with colds and viruses, so the threat of a seizure was always lurking around the corner. The seizures were absolutely horrifying, and each time I thought my son was dying. Oh, those were long, hard years.

One positive result of Guy's health issues was that for the first time in our marriage, we began attending church as a family. I had quit attending church when I left home. Scott had grown up nominally Catholic. While he believed in the Father, Son, and Holy Spirit, he hadn't grown up praying, attending church regularly, or pursuing a personal relationship with Jesus. But when Guy began his horrifying seizures, we started praying together over our children at bedtime. Desperate for hope, healing, and a church family, we also began attending Calvary Chapel in Denver. While we didn't make any close friends there, the church quickly became our life-support system, and we felt deeply encouraged as to God's tremendous love for both of us and our little family.

Still, the spirit of fear had settled in and made itself at home in my soul. Buffeted, weak, and powerless, I felt completely helpless to the enemy's intrusion, a victim of circumstances. I'd completely forgotten that as a believer in Jesus Christ I had any authority against this enemy. I remember telling my father, "Dad, I've been in countless perilous situations. I've had three car accidents. I've been scuba-diving with sharks and skydiving out of perfectly good airplanes many times. But I've never known true terror until I had children!"

Even worse, that spirit of fear transformed me into a controlling nut job. God created me with strong leadership abilities. But fear changed me into someone I never want to be again, easily frustrated and with extremely high expectations of everyone around me— myself, Scott, the hired help, including my older sister Ashley, who came to live with us as our nanny the last six months of my full-time employment.

Ashley would jokingly refer to me as General Patton, the WW2 allied commander infamous for his hard-driving personality. I didn't think it was very funny, but I could see the similarities. I made home uncomfortable for Scott and for Ashley while she nannied for us. They both felt they had to walk on eggshells around me and could never do anything well enough to please me. I in turn was so controlled by fear I just didn't know any other way to get through each day and take care of my children as best I could.

Life or Death Are in the Power of the Tongue

Dad wasn't the only person to whom I proclaimed my fear. Looking back, I see that I gave fear a voice. Worse, I allowed fear's voice to speak much more often and louder than the Word of Truth. It is natural to be fearful about a baby when terrifying circumstances are present. But instead of flipping out and getting swept away by the tide, we need an effective battle strategy.

We'll be talking in-depth later about a spiritual battle plan. But here is where my strategy failed. I didn't give voice to the power of God over baby Guy's health. I didn't begin decreeing God's promises over our son's life until well after the fear had rooted in my heart. I knew the promises of God's Word. But our enemy made fear seem normal as though it was simply part and parcel of the circumstances I was walking through.

Because I didn't know what the answers were or how to move forward or how to protect my children, I became a victim to fear. Make that completely obsessed by fear. Within a matter of months, I had two battles on my hands: the health of my son and the peace of my mind. I was outgunned, outmatched, and outnumbered, just the way the devil likes it! Ephesians 6:12 gives us a clear picture of that battle.

> For our struggle is not against flesh and blood, but against the rulers, against the authorities, against the powers of this dark world and against the spiritual forces of evil in the heavenly realms.

Takeaway

Here are my big takeaways from this excruciatingly extended experience. First, don't come into agreement with medical diagnoses by using language such as "he has an issue with seizures . . . he is bipolar . . . the doctor says my cancer could come back . . . her diabetes is driving her crazy!" Rather than pinning a medical label on ourselves or loved ones, try this alternative: "We've been given a diagnosis of XYZ that we do not accept, and we would like everyone to stand with us in prayer over that situation."

Second, don't research online for hours figuring out what could go wrong. Okay, yes, you can ask me how I know not to do this!

Third, do not rely on how you *feel* about the circumstances to set your internal compass. Feelings are emotions and are easily swayed. Instead follow the wise advice the Holy Spirit gives us through the apostle Paul's letter to the Philippian church.

> Do not be anxious about anything, but in every situation, by prayer and petition, with thanksgiving,

> present your requests to God. And the peace of God,
> which transcends all understanding, will guard your
> hearts and your minds in Christ Jesus. (Philippians
> 4:6-7)

Which brings me to my final and most significant takeaway from this experience. We saw above that our battle is not physical but spiritual. And so are our weapons, as the apostle Paul explains.

> The weapons we fight with are not the weapons of
> the world. On the contrary, they have divine power
> to demolish strongholds. We demolish arguments
> and every pretension that sets itself up against the
> knowledge of God, and we take captive every thought
> to make it obedient to Christ. (2 Corinthians 10:4-5)

And our chief weapon is our sword, which is God's Word.

> Take the helmet of salvation and the sword of the
> Spirit, which is the word of God. (Ephesians 6:17)

> For the word of God is alive and active. Sharper
> than any double-edged sword, it penetrates even to
> dividing soul and spirit, joints and marrow; it judges
> the thoughts and attitudes of the heart. (Hebrews
> 4:12)

In other words, God's spirit-breathed Word gives us all the ammunition we need to slay fear. God says about the words He gives us in the Bible, which is our weapon against Satan and his spirit of fear:

> Don't lose sight of them. Let them penetrate deep
> into your heart, for they bring life to those who find
> them, and healing to their whole body. (Proverbs
> 4:21-22, NLT)

With that assurance, it is urgent we give God's promises made available to us by our Redeemer Christ Jesus a louder, more frequent voice over what the spirit of fear is saying. How? Every time a fearful thought or comment springs up, combat it with powerful healing promises and decrees from the Scriptures. This crushes the enemy's threats and brings our hearts and minds into alignment with the power in God's Word. With boldness, we can claim over our loved ones, the words of Jesus to His disciples.

> Truly I say to you, whatever you bind on earth shall have been bound in heaven; and whatever you loose on earth shall have been loosed in heaven. (Matthew 18:18, NASB)

CHAPTER TWELVE

INHERITANCE

"In him you also, when you heard the word of truth, the gospel of your salvation, and believed in him, were sealed with the promised Holy Spirit, who is the guarantee of our inheritance until we acquire possession of it, to the praise of his glory."

EPHESIANS 1:13-14 (ESV)

I only wish I'd known these vital spiritual principles at the time. Thankfully, God is loving and patient, even when I insisted on learning life lessons the hard way. Though God's loving patience was not something I really grasped then. My concept of a heavenly Father remained a harsh, stern judge just waiting for my next inevitable slip-up again to lower the boom of punishment.

By this point, Scott and I had agreed that I should let my career go for a season to focus on being a full-time mom. Once Guy was healthier and in school, I could start my career back up again. This would just be for a few short years, so no big deal.

Except to me it *was* a big deal. It meant laying down my identity of self-made me. Relinquishing control and the safety of my own future and destiny. Giving up the Kingdom of Ami I'd worked so hard to build. I'd always determined that I'd never stop working. Now I had to lay it all aside to be a stay-at-home mom.

To complicate matters, we had absolutely no support system around us, a dangerous place to be in our circumstances. Scott had never known any support system other than his mom, and even that didn't include deep, healthy discussions on important topics. My family lived nearly a thousand miles away. All we had was each other.

It didn't help that we drank frequently and still hadn't learned to communicate well. I needed booze for the courage to broach tough topics, and Scott would sometimes react with hurtful, harsh language that felt a painful flashback to my dad's angry speech. And unlike in childhood, I didn't meekly shut up but answered in kind. The chasm between us widened further.

But in the midst of the pain and worry and a troubled marriage, God used one person in my life to touch my heart and draw me back to himself—my sister Ashley.

Eight years older than me, Ashley had endured her own trauma of abuse from my father. She'd struggled with learning delays in school, partly because fear of my dad's extreme reaction to any poor grades led to panic attacks that further impacted her ability to perform academically. He punished her mercilessly for any failure to perform. Ashley like the rest of my older siblings had escaped from our household by the time I reached my teens. But unlike me, she'd never turned her back on God or doubted her faith. In fact, during the years that I'd pursued an extremely worldly lifestyle, she'd become an ordained minister.

My children loved Auntie Ashley. Since Elsa and Guy were babies, she'd visited us in Denver when she could, and they were delighted to have her move in full-time as their nanny. From her own spiritual journey and theological studies, she introduced me to a concept completely new and foreign to me—the gospel of grace.

At first I had no idea what she was talking about and was at the very least skeptical if not a bit angry for what appeared to me was false doctrine. After all, we'd been raised to understand that God was a God of judgment who expected absolute obedience, submission, and perfection from his followers. Any shortfall in meeting God's standards merited and could be expected to engender harsh punishment. Our only hope was constant profound repentance and ensuring that transgressions were not repeated. In other words, God the Father was not much different as a parent than my earthly father.

So when Ashley began sharing the unprecedented message of grace she'd been studying and listening to as well as the love of a heavenly Father exemplified to us through Christ, I was at first incensed.

"How can this be true?" I would argue with her. "Are you

suggesting we've been wrong all this time? That we've been lied to all our lives?"

Patiently, she would show me in Scripture and explain to me the differences between what we'd been taught and what God's Word actually demonstrated about the love of Christ. And gradually, Ashley's words began opening blinders the enemy wanted to remain shut. I still had a long way to go. While I was now attending church, reading my Bible, and praying, I struggled with worry and fear for my children, resentment over the loss of my identity as a successful careerwoman, anger towards my husband, and the conviction I'd never be good enough to earn God's favor.

But slowly, like healing ointment on a painful wound, like gentle rain on parched ground, the truth of God's grace and mercy began permeating my hard, angry spirit. I began remembering God's love for me that I'd felt as a small child. His mercy in healing my bone tumor. His protection during all the reckless years I'd ignored him. I was stunned that God would still want me and could still love me after the lifestyle I'd lived and all I'd done. But that I had a heavenly Father who loved me and whose desire for my life was to pour out grace and mercy, not punishment and judgement, was something I no longer doubted. There was no greater gift my sister could have given me, and I will never stop thanking God for her.

Understand Your Inheritance

As I came to understand God's grace, love, and mercy in place of the harsh judgement that had been my image of a heavenly Father, I also began learning what it meant to be adopted into God's family. Not just the hope of eternal life in heaven instead of eternal punishment for my sins in hell, but a heritage NOW as daughter of the King of kings. Let's look at just a few of the many inheritances promises we have available to enjoy NOW as title-bearing sons and daughters of God.

There are plenty of Scriptures that describe all that we have as children of God, and I recommend doing an entire word study on the topic. But for now we are going to look at one single passage that lists so many inheritance promises that in itself it gives a comprehensive summary.

> The **Spirit you received** does not make you slaves, so that you live in fear again; rather, the Spirit you received brought about your **adoption to sonship**. And by him we cry, "**Abba, Father.**" The Spirit himself testifies with our spirit that we are **God's children**. Now if we are children, then we are heirs—**heirs of God and co-heirs with Christ**, if indeed we share in his sufferings in order that we may also **share in his glory**. I consider that our present sufferings are not worth comparing with the **glory that will be revealed in us**. For the creation waits in eager expectation for the children of God to be revealed . . . in hope that the creation itself will be liberated from its bondage to decay and brought into the **freedom and glory of the children of God** . . . What, then, shall we say in response to these things? If **God is for us**, who can be against us? He who did not spare his own Son, but gave him up for us all— how will he not also, along with him, **graciously give us all things**? Who will bring any charge against those whom God has chosen? It is **God who justifies**. Who then is the one who condemns? No one. Christ Jesus who died—more than that, who was raised to life—is at the right hand of God and is also **interceding for us** . . . No, in all these things we are **more than conquerors** through him who loved us. For I am convinced that neither death nor life, neither angels nor demons, neither the present nor the future, nor any powers, neither height nor depth, nor anything else in all creation, will be able

to separate us from **the love of God that is in Christ Jesus our Lord.** (Romans 8:15-39)

Wow! Even the above passage is only part of the entire description of all we have in Christ, so I hope you will take time to read the entire chapter. But just look at a few of our entitlements as God's sons and daughters.

We have received the Holy Spirit. This means that as a Christian, a child of God, you have the very same Spirit of God living and breathing in you who lived in Jesus as Jesus walked on this earth, fully God and fully man. It is the same Spirit who gave Jesus the power to heal the sick, raise the dead, cleanse the lepers, and cast out demons. The same Spirit who inspired the people who wrote the Bible and continuously breathes the breath of God into the Word of God, giving life to the Word and life to all those who consume the Word. That is why in Christ you are so powerful. You have the same Spirit who raised Christ from the dead. You have the wonder-working, miracle-working power of God in you.

We are adopted into sonship. Notice, by the way, the alternative mentioned in the above passage. We could have been taken into God's household as a servant (literally, a slave, as much a possession as a farm animal), living in fear of what our master might do to us if we displease him. A servitude of fear is what Satan wants for us. Instead, we are adopted as a beloved child with such a close relationship with our heavenly Father we call him the intimate "**Abba**" or Daddy.

Now, I like being a woman, but I LOVE being a SON! Let me clarify that God is certainly not gender biased. He's me (and you!) biased. But sonship, whether we are male or female, references in this context a special position of belonging. There is an inherent title transfer and authority that goes with being a direct descendent on the male lineage. That special position is that of **joint heirs with Christ**, Son of God and our adoptive Brother.

Which means that Christ's own inheritance in heaven is also ours. We are forever seated (dwelling) in Christ at the right hand (the side of adjudication, justice and peace) of the Father (Ephesians

2:6). All that is under Jesus's feet is under our feet. That includes fear, torment, dis-order and dis-ease! As we pray, **he intercedes on our behalf**, so we pray from a position of victory, not as a victim!

Because we are joint heirs, we also share his **glory**. Imagine having the glory of the Son of God revealed in us. **We have freedom**, and whom the Son sets free is free indeed (John 8:36)! Our heavenly Father himself has **justified** us. How? The judgment and sentence for our ALL sins, past, present and future, have already been administered, carried out, and paid by the spotless Lamb of God. This means that **condemnation is no more**. We are forever in right-standing (righteous) with our Father, inheritors of his Spirit.

Because we are in right-standing, we are now and forever more in communion with our heavenly Father. He is not looking for excuses to punish us but looking for excuses to bless us. **He is for us,** not against us. He's not angry with us but happy with us. More than that, our heavenly Father **loves us so much** that nothing in heaven and earth—not life, death, angels, demons, or anything else we can imagine—can cause him not to love us.

If that wasn't enough, **God graciously gives us all things.** Wow, again! That means everything in heaven and on earth is part of our inheritance. Including access to all the love, compassion, peace, grace, authority, and power that Jesus demonstrated on earth. And it is because of that inheritance that we are—not will be, not hope to be, not are working towards being—we *are* **more than conquerors**. Again, not because of anything we've done or are capable of doing, but because of Whose we are. Because of our identity and inheritance as daughters and sons and joint heirs of Almighty God.

"But how is any of this possible?" you may be asking.

I'm glad you asked! As my dear sister Ashley so patiently communicated to me, it is by grace that our wonderful inheritance is given and it is by grace we receive (Ephesians 2:8-10).

"But that makes no sense!" you might argue as I once did.

I KNOW! Isn't it GREAT?! It is by God's love that salvation was paid for us, and by his love and grace alone that the Holy Spirit, the

Spirit of our living Savior inside of us, fans the flames of God's holy Word to life inside us!

All that "good news" is still hard for me to grasp. I don't know about you, but I'd never experienced this teaching in all my years. It is incredibly liberating, empowering, and exciting, isn't it?! If we aren't standing on the truth of the gospel of Jesus as the apostle Paul taught it in this passage, we are missing the true value of Christ's finished work at the cross.

Already, do you see how you can move from talking about the fear-mongering giants in your life to moving them out of your life? As a child of the Most High, you pray, decree, and command from a place of victory, of position, of authority. Here's the truth. To *not* command from a position of authority in Jesus Christ shortchanges his finished work at the cross.

Come on, say it with me and with boldness: "Not on my watch!"
Hallelujah!

ACTIVITY I: What Is Your Identity?

Two of my favorite authors on these topics are Leif Hetland and Joseph Prince. I highly recommend *Called to Reign* by Leif Hetland and *The Power of Right Believing* by Joseph Prince. Both are awesome resources to have on hand. Leif's website **globalmissionsawareness. com** also has several MP3 download sermons that have been battle changers for me. May I recommend you listen to "Healing the Orphan Spirit" and "Which Chair are You Sitting In?" Then consider the following questions and jot down any thoughts that come to mind.

How would you define your identity before today?

_____

_____

_____

_____

_____

How would you define your identity now?

_____

_____

_____

_____

CHAPTER THIRTEEN

DISTRACTION

*"Stay alert! Watch out for your great enemy, the devil. He prowls
around like a roaring lion, looking for someone to devour."*

1 PETER 5:8 NLT

Sadly, even when we are making spiritual strides forward, Satan
is always on the prowl to catch us off guard. His work is most
effective when we're tired or distracted with emotions like worry or
bitterness, which certainly described Scott and me. These are prime
conditions for a spiritual attack, and the enemy had been working
overtime to ensure that distractions in the form of attraction outside
of marriage were in front of both of us.

I was confronted with an opportunity of the male persuasion
who found me very attractive. The attraction was mutual. Instead of
being on high alert and guarding my heart, I began looking forward
to encountering him again. Just thinking about him and how much
he was attracted to me made my head spin and heart beat wildly.
Thankfully, God in his mercy protected me from finding out what
could have happened next.

Then in December 2014, Satan struck again completely out
of left field. The children and I had traveled to Arkansas during
the Christmas school break to visit my extended family, many of
whom still lived there. We stayed with Ashley, who was being "Super
Auntie" while I recuperated from a painful surgical procedure.

Scott joined us over Christmas. I immediately noticed that
something was different. He was more withdrawn and quieter than
usual. Some of my family members noticed it also and voiced their
concerns. With my recuperation from surgery, I was too tired to
care. But once we'd all returned home after Christmas, I mentioned
it to Scott.

"Nothing's wrong," he commented pleasantly. "I've just been busy, I guess."

He'd been polite enough, if very aloof. But I knew something wasn't right, though there was nothing I could really put my finger on. Still, with two small children, one with special needs, a household to run, and my own night-time drinking habit, I was too busy to launch an investigation.

To make a long and deeply painful story short, just two weeks later Scott confessed to having an inappropriate relationship with a female colleague. I was stunned and furious. That I'd come close to the same transgression didn't enter my thinking. After all, I hadn't followed through, had I? That without this crisis I too might have eventually transgressed was a thought I refused to even entertain. There was only one sinner here, and it wasn't me!

I was so furious I suddenly realized I had a loaded handgun nearby (this was Colorado!) and that I was raging enough to fantasize about blowing this man's head off his shoulders. This scared me enough to bring my emotions somewhat under control. But I felt absolutely shattered. I'd grown up in an unhappy home, and to me my crowning achievement, the "kingdom of Ami" I'd so painstakingly built, was completely wrapped up in attaining the loving marriage and happy home my own parents had never achieved.

For me this was not just a betrayal but a devastating blow from which I didn't see how I could ever recover. It broke me. It broke my heart. It broke my spirit. Like a calving glacier, all the safety and security I'd carefully laid around my life and family had been sheared away, leaving me feeling completely naked and exposed. Our little family was broken, and there seemed zero hope of it ever being whole again.

To add to the shock, pain, and betrayal, we were right in the middle of another cross-country move from Denver, Colorado, to Boca Raton, Florida. In fact, we'd been praying for a relocation for over a year. Having two small children; one with special needs, far away from any family and any established network of friends had proved very lonely and confining. We were more than ready for the move back to familiar surroundings, warm weather, family within easier driving distance, and friends.

It should have been a warning sign that Scott had shown little enthusiasm when this particular job opportunity in Florida came along. In fact, he'd told me, "We don't have to move to Florida. I can telecommute for this job."

Now I was grateful to God, who'd laid the plans for this move long before the crisis that had ripped our family apart. I just wanted to get far away from Denver as quickly as possible and settle my children somewhere safe.

"Just get there and let the dust settle," I told myself. "Then I'll be able to figure it out."

Our scheduled move was just two weeks after my discovery. Whatever issues our marriage faced, Scott was committed to his children and wanted the best for his family. So he agreed to break off the relationship once and for all. I wanted to protect my children and foster a healthy relationship between them and their father, so I chose to believe him.

Saying goodbye to the home we'd created together and loved was heartbreaking. The night before our flight to Florida, we—a shattered family of four—stayed in a hotel near the Denver airport. The room had two queen beds. Scott slept in one with our son while I slept with our daughter in the other. As I cuddled Elsa close, I had little hope our life as a family would ever be the same again. All I could do was pray. For protection for our children. For peace, which seemed so far out of reach. For hope of a future that didn't include a fractured family. Heartsick and in pain, I slept fitfully for a few hours.

Early the next morning, we took our innocent, trusting little ones by their tiny hands and boarded the plane for our non-stop flight to Fort Lauderdale. Scott and I spoke to each other only when necessary and were polite and businesslike in our conversation. As we settled into our seats, I stole one glance at Scott, who was looking out the window. I saw him take a deep breath, close his eyes, and rub his head as if in disbelief.

I wondered what he was thinking. Was it disbelief over how much destruction he'd left in our jet-stream? Uncertainty? Despair and loss over leaving this other relationship? He wasn't going to say, and I wasn't going to ask!

Landing in Fort Lauderdale, we drove to Boca Raton. We had rented a furnished apartment there on a six-month lease, originally with the idea of taking our time to find a more permanent home. The master bedroom had a king-sized bed. On our first full day there, we tucked our little ones into bed for their afternoon naps, then lay down to rest. Scott lay on one side while I lay on the other. I breathed deeply and steadily, trying to quieten the thundering noise of my heartache that banged away in my temples and ears.

"I can't do this, God," I cried out silently. "I don't know what to do, but I can't do any of it."

Be still. Rest. Be quiet. Rest. With each breath, my head willed my body to rest. Rolling to one side, I stared across the room at the closet doors. *Be still. Be still.*

All of a sudden, I felt a hand on my back. The pressure was steady and firm. My first assumption was that the hand was Scott's.

Oh, no! my heart thundered. *He wants to apologize and reconcile. I can't! I don't want to! What do I say? How will I respond?*

I didn't turn over immediately to face my husband, still not sure how to respond. Finally, I took a deep breath and rolled over on my other side to face him. I found him fast asleep, flat on his back, arms folded across his chest.

How can he sleep so easily? I could have gnashed my teeth to powder to see him lying there so calmly and peacefully. Then I suddenly grasped that the hand I'd felt on my back couldn't have been Scott's. My realization shifted from "That wasn't his hand?" to "That wasn't Scott's hand! That was *His* hand! God's hand!"

Now I don't know about you, but ordinarily I'd be ecstatic to know that the Creator of all, God himself, deemed me worthy enough to transcend time and space to manifest a physical touch on my back. I was ever so thankful, of course, and still am. But at that moment I felt so heartsick I couldn't get excited.

Rolling back over to face the closet, I whispered, "Okay, Lord, what do you have for me?"

In that instant, God gave me a vision of me being shot up high on a giant water fountain like those you see sometimes in ornate hotel courtyards or plazas. Far below, I could see Scott holding little Guy in one arm and little Elsa by the hand.

"What does it mean, Lord?" I asked.

"Daughter, I'm raising you up, far above the circumstances." God's Spirit whispered gently to my heart. "You'll see."

I didn't feel particularly different as I lay there beside my sleeping husband on that king-sized bed. The feelings of rejection, and trauma didn't magically disappear. I was still in excruciating pain.

But I now had a promise. A whisper of peace in the storm. Abba, Father God, had esteemed me important enough to meet me right where I was. To place his hand physically on my back so I could be still and know that he is God.

I would return to that vision hundreds of times over the next three years. It was a couple of years later that God showed me where to trace the vision to its corresponding scripture and message hand-selected for me.

> Because he set his love on Me, therefore I will save him. I will set him [securely] on high because he knows My name [he confidently trusts and relies on Me, knowing I will never abandon him, no, never]. (Psalms 91:14, Amplified Bible)

What a God. What a Father! That's our Papa!

CHAPTER FOURTEEN

GRIEF

"The Lord is near the brokenhearted and saves
those who are crushed in spirit."

PSALMS 34:18

Over the next several months, Scott and I both recognized that our marriage was an epic failure. We sought professional counseling, but there was only so much even a professional could do. During one session, the therapist pointed at me and said I was "stuck" in the pain and unforgiveness.

"Ya' THINK?!" I wanted to shout at her. "So I should just buck up like a good little camper, right?!"

Those close friends we'd thought we had and even family members on Scott's side faded from our lives. We were just too broken and too messy for others to want to maintain a relationship with us. My family, who all lived in Arkansas and Missouri, did maintain contact and visited as frequently as possible.

Other than that, we were all alone. It all hurt so bad and the loss of security and safety was so severe that I completely imploded. I could barely function or hold even a part-time job. In the old days, this phenomenon was called a nervous breakdown. I truly thought I'd die still trying to hold my sanity together for the sake of the children.

I finally insisted Scott move out. A colleague from his new job let Scott stay with him temporarily. We tried to keep things as normal as possible for the children, so Scott would come over each evening to tuck them in and say evening prayers with them. The situation was extremely uncomfortable for both of us. Scott was uneasy around me—and with good reason since I was still as furiously angry as when I'd refrained from pulling out a gun in Colorado. In truth, the weapon was safely away in storage, but I was even scared of myself that I might just blow.

Scott would then head over to his colleague's home for the night—usually with a stop at a bar first—and I'd be left alone with the kids. I was barely keeping a lid on my grief and pain, which along with the anger was mixed with growing panic about what the future held. Our separation had lasted less than a week when I just couldn't take it any longer. I asked Scott to spend the night with the kids so I could get away to stay overnight at a friend's house.

But despite plenty of alcohol, my friend's company couldn't numb the pain. She tried to encourage me as best she could, reminding me, "Sure it's rough now! But you are strong and smart, and you're going to get through this."

It didn't help. The whole evening, I couldn't shake deep grief that whispered to me, *I should have been kinder to him. We should have been kinder to each other. We should have looked for opportunities to be kinder, softer, gentler. We could have been kinder.*

Once I was alone in my friend's guest bedroom, I cried all night. I barely slept and continued crying all the next morning until I returned to our apartment. Still crying, I repeated those grieving phrases to Scott.

Scott in turn begged my forgiveness. Fervently, he told me, "If you will just take me back, I promise that you will never be sorry."

Scott moved back home that very afternoon. What I didn't know until some months later was that Scott had experienced his own supernatural encounter during our separation. At the time, I was in such turmoil I might not have believed it if he'd told me. But now I certainly do!

Scott's Description of His Encounter with Jesus.

I was staying with a coworker I'd only recently met, basically feeling my life was over. This was the lowest time in my life, and I was honestly contemplating just ending it all. I'd reached the point of looking up my life insurance policy to ensure it would pay out in the event of a suicide. Ultimately, I knew I couldn't go that route for fear of what it would do to my children. I didn't want them spending their lives wondering why I'd done it and if it was somehow their fault.

On this particular Saturday evening, I decided to get out of the apartment and walk over to the closest bar. My coworker didn't even want to go with me, probably because I was just so toxic. I sat at the bar, not looking around or talking to anyone except the bartender to order one vodka after another. As the night wore on, even that interaction devolved to just glancing up to get the bartender's attention and motioning to my empty glass for another refill.

I'm not sure how many drinks I had, how long I stayed, or even how I got back to the apartment. My next recollection was being woken up out of a dead sleep. I sat up and looked around, not sure how or why I was up. I then looked straight ahead. Out of nowhere, someone was standing right in front of me. A bright light came from behind him or perhaps was emanating out of him. Though I couldn't see his face, I knew who it was—Jesus! I sat there frozen, unable to move or say a word.

Then Jesus said, "Do not give up, my son. Do not give up. It is not over yet. Do not give up."

I felt warm and joyous and totally at peace. Then as suddenly as he'd appeared, the brightly-lit figure was gone. I just sat there on the edge of the bed, basking in this feeling of warmth and happiness. When I eventually took a look at the time, it was 5am. Since it was so early, I figured I should go back to sleep, but I couldn't. I just lay there enjoying that wonderful feeling that seemed to linger in the room. I didn't want to leave. I knew then that Jesus had come to save me. Not just the whole world in general, but me personally. Me who didn't deserve saving or mercy. At that moment, I knew that somehow, some way it was all going to be okay.

ACTIVITY J: What Are Your Battles?

I've been talking a lot about my own battles, whether the fear I grew up with or my marriage problems. Your life battles may look very much like mine or very different. Regardless of what battles you are facing, you need a battle plan, as we will be formulating later. But to create an effective plan, first you need to know what battles you are fighting and how effective your current plan is. Take a few minutes to think about the following questions and jot down the answers that come to mind. There are no wrong answers here, so be as comprehensive as you can. If you need more space, jot down answers in a notebook or journal.

What are your daily and/or life battles?

_____

_____

_____

How successful have you been fighting these battles? Write down any successes that come to mind as these may help in planning effective battle strategies.

_____

_____

_____

_____

CHAPTER FIFTEEN

ANXIETY

"And we all, with unveiled face, beholding the glory of the Lord, are being transformed into the same image from one degree of glory to another. For this comes from the Lord who is the Spirit."

2 CORINTHIANS 3:18 ESV

But it wasn't as easy as just expressing forgiveness and moving back in with each other. Scott had said I'd never be sorry if I took him back. In truth, over the following months I was often sorry.

For one, mouthing forgiveness was easier than learning to trust again. Scott and I worked towards more transparency, making sure we both had full access to each other's emails and phone messages. We continued with marriage counseling. We began attending as a family the church we still attend today. While I still didn't know about Scott's own divine encounter, we both recognized we needed God in our lives and a loving church family.

At the same time, therapy wasn't really helping. That day I'd felt God's touch on my back, God had given me a promise that he would lift me up above my circumstances. He'd also given me that incredible vision of being carried high on a soaring fountain to hold in my heart and recount and recall. But there was a deep valley to cross. I'd lost faith in the sanctuary of our marriage. I'd lost hope that our marriage would ever be redeemable.

As for love? Certainly not on my own! I remained in a constant low boil of anger, and without a miracle from God, to even think of loving Scott again seemed impossible.

For his part, Scott had agreed to try to salvage our marriage. But to my perspective, he seemed to be just plodding through duties and obligations of work and family life. Marriage counselors typically want to counsel toward the unity and continuation of the marriage.

But the reality was that Scott and I were both so faulty we needed individual healing first. Inevitably, the therapist would turn to me with some comment like, "Ami, it feels like you're stuck. Do you want to move forward in this marriage?"

Which again felt as though I was being given sole blame for our marriage problems. When we did communicate, we were often sniping unkindly at each other. However hard I tried to forget the past, the trauma of betrayal, abandonment, and rejection compounded by the trauma of my childhood was an excruciating daily pain. I thought I'd be crushed to death by it.

We finally quit marriage counseling after three separate therapists had resulted in no help at all. Scott and I were both drinking to dangerous excess, and one day Scott even missed his return flight home from a business trip because he'd been drinking heavily enough he'd overslept. I was ready to throw in the towel entirely. But Scott again asked for my forgiveness and promised to quit drinking.

To my astonishment, he kept that promise (unlike myself at that time since I was still drinking!). To this day, he hasn't had another drink. He also shared with me his experience with Jesus. To be honest, I was skeptical of his story. Only much later—and after God's great grace and mercy to both of us—did I come to realize he was telling me the truth.

To make matters worse, all this anger, fear, and pain intensified into full-blown panic attacks. Along with the panic attacks came an onslaught of physiological issues, including a dysfunctional thyroid, and great physical pain in my body, particularly my neck. My family doctor told me I had an anxiety disorder and was suffering from PTSD (Post Traumatic Stress Disorder). I couldn't care less what it was called. I just wanted it to go away. Or at least lift a little bit so I could draw a breath and think clearly. I'd been prescribed Xanax for the anxiety, but it made me feel too wonky to care for my children, who were just three and four at this time, so I used it only in the middle of lengthy panic attacks.

The Physiology of Anxiety

If you've never dealt with anxiety disorder or PTSD, you might be saying, "Well, fear, anxiety, depression—that's just a part of life. Ignore it long enough and it'll go away." Or "Don't be a wimp! Just toughen up!"

If so, you would not be alone. Too much of western society still believes the same. But I can assure you it is not a normal part of life. Nor will it go away if just ignored. This extended season in which I experienced unrelenting panic attacks remains my darkest hour. The physiological condition diagnosed was "anxiety disorder." In the past, it was more commonly termed a nervous breakdown.

In this condition and in scenarios of PTSD, the brain does a most horrible thing to help the body survive. It cyclically dumps cortisol, adrenaline, noradrenaline, and other stress-related hormones into the body. This provides the body with massive energy resources in preparation for the "fight, flight, or freeze" process we discussed clear back in the first chapter. During this process, neurons are disengaged from the prefrontal cortex of the brain.

Here's the twist. The prefrontal cortex is the region of the brain responsible for most of our executive functions such as planning, problem-solving, reasoning, and decision-making. In other words, all the important stuff! Anxiety disengages neurons in the prefrontal cortex linked to decision-making, rendering it nearly useless. Under the effects of anxiety, the important reasoning and decision-making stuff gets relocated to the basement of the brain we typically never use. Okay, I'm paraphrasing the actual science in that last sentence. But it is a cruel reality.

In an article published by *Psychology Today* magazine, "How Does Anxiety Short Circuit the Decision-Making Process?" (Mar 17, 2016), world-class endurance athlete, author, coach, and public health advocate Christopher Bergland states:

> Anxiety is such a prominent and debilitating component of most psychiatric disorders. Anxiety

is often a key player in major depressive disorder (MDD), post-traumatic stress disorder (PTSD), schizophrenia, obsessive compulsive disorders (OCD), and addiction.

Here's the picture of anxiety disorder. Jumpiness at sudden movements and loud noises. Fearful scenes flying across the imagination. Cycles of panic for no apparent reason. Gasping for air like a guppy out of water. Just straight up terror. Logical reasoning and decision-making gone. Ability to remember anything toast; often real physical pain to boot.

If this applies to you, no, you are not crazy. Nor are you going crazy. This is only a season. There is an end to this, and the end of your trouble is in sight. Even if you do not see it, your Abba does, and the blood of Jesus assures it.

We will get to that soon, I promise you.

CHAPTER SIXTEEN

PANIC

*"You will not fear the terror of night, nor the arrow
that flies by day, nor the pestilence that stalks in the
darkness, nor the plague that destroys at midday."*

PSALMS 91:5-6

But first to finish my own confession. For more than two years, my life was wrought with pain and torment. I was terrified of everything and everyone. I was still unable to trust Scott, the security of our marriage, or the safety of our children. When anxiety wasn't ruling the moment, guilt was. The Enemy kept whispering into my ears condemnation for my many shortcomings as a parent of two small children as well as the demise of a marriage that still seemed doomed for divorce court. Every single day seemed chock-full of danger and hazard.

Some days the panic attacks were so frequent and intense I was terrified I'd die and leave my children motherless. On the flip side, remaining alive didn't seem particularly attractive either. All I could see ahead of me was a bleak future of a failed marriage and raising two children on my own alone in my bitterness and pain. No matter which way my thoughts led me, I would quickly find myself overwhelmed by yet another panic attack.

It is hard to describe just how awful those attacks felt. From the moment I peeled myself out of bed to make breakfast for the children until I poured myself medication from a wine bottle after they were tucked into bed, I felt forever tormented. I would drink myself numb and stumble to bed. But even falling asleep felt like I was falling out of control straight into hell.

Daytime hours were a dizzying array of questions, emotional pain, and a literal physical feeling that I was dying. My throat held a constant lump. My heartbeat was a fast-pounding bass drum, deafening in my ears, while my lungs couldn't draw in enough air. The devil would whisper in my ear, "Your throat's closing up, Ami, most likely from throat cancer. Your heart rate is way too high. Is that pain in your right arm under the collarbone? It's probably a heart attack. Makes sense. How appropriate!"

All this happened several times a day. People liked to encourage, "Take it day by day, honey, day by day." But I was living moment by wretched, gagging moment. I often thought "this must be what hell is like."

Looking back, I realize that there were undoubtedly other loving Christians and even pastoral staff within our Boca Raton church family who would have been more than willing to offer help if they'd known how much we were struggling. But we were very new to the church, and we never asked them to help. The way I figured it, if professional therapists couldn't help us, certainly no one else in the church was equipped to handle our hot mess!

Finally, one panic attack was so bad it landed me in the emergency room. Scott and I had taken our daughter Elsa to Disney World in Orlando for her sixth birthday. As we headed home, traffic was bumper to bumper on the turnpike. Scott moderately stepped on the brake to avoid bumping into the car in front of us. But in my mind's eye, he'd slammed on the brake, leaving skid marks on the road. Of course this wasn't truly the case. But terror had taken my brain's engine hostage, and the pistons were firing on all cylinders.

Ping! Snap! The ticking time-bomb of unspoken pain and unanswered questions in my mind exploded, and I went off. The evil spirit of fear hissed out hot and fast like a deflating balloon, fully engaging the panic button, as Pandora's box of accusations came flying out of my mouth. "Why would you take chances with your family? Why would you put their lives at risk? How can you make decisions that will put them in danger and allow them to be hurt? How dare you!"

I finally demanded that Scott pull over so I could "walk it off" on the shoulder of that very busy turnpike. Completely hysterical and desperate for peace, I started praying, gasping, sobbing, hyperventilating, and praying some more. Then I suddenly realized that my hands felt all tingly.

"Something's happening to my hands!" I got out in a strangled voice to Scott through the open front passenger window.

My hands went from tingling to contorting into the shape of beast-like claws. By now I was terrified that I was having a stroke right in front of my children. My panic increased as my arms began to spontaneously draw up and pin themselves to my chest, claw-hands and all.

Scott called 911, and shortly thereafter I founded myself loaded onto a gurney and carted off in an ambulance to the nearest E.R. Climbing back into our vehicle, Scott and the children followed the ambulance to the hospital, where they remained with me until the drama trauma was sorted out. No, I wasn't dying or stroking out. It was just a raging panic attack.

About a year later at my routine annual physical exam, the nurse checked my blood pressure, remarking that it was a little high. I immediately panicked. She waited briefly, then checked it again on the alternate arm. Ka-pow! Up went the already high blood pressure.

"Just breathe! Be calm!" I commanded myself as the nurse exited the exam room, looking worried.

A few moments later, the doctor came in. By now my heart was thundering away in my chest, so when the doctor rechecked my blood pressure, it had soared to new heights. The doctor sent me straight to the E.R. After a few hours of testing and observation, the doctor on duty in the E.R. concluded that I had "white-coat syndrome." This is a learned behavior from associating anxiety-provoking experiences to doctors.

I made no response to the diagnosis, but inside I was thinking, "Oh, Doc, if you only knew how totally scrambled up my wiring is, you'd probably send me to the psych ward!"

Anxiety Is Not Our Inheritance

Now, I know that I'm not the only one who has gone through such an experience. I'm guessing some who might be reading this book have experienced anxiety, even panic attacks. If you are walking through a season of severe anxiety right now, I just want to take some time to address you. I may not know you, but I know the pain and torment you are walking through. Tears are streaming right now from my eyes as I say to you that I am so sorry!

But please believe me that this isn't happening because God doesn't care about you and wants to punish you. You are under attack by the evil one, not your loving heavenly Father. And those fiery darts being thrown at you by Satan cannot defeat you. Through this book, I want to help you raise your shield of faith in Jesus's mighty name (Ephesians 6:16).

May I recommend that in this season you don't try to figure anything right now or map out your future. Your only order of business at this moment is to heal. Handle only what is essential for you, your family and your job, but let the focus be healing for you. I promise you, this season will not last forever. Hopefully, not nearly as long as it did for me. I didn't have an understanding of my identity, purpose, and inheritance in Christ or a battle plan to help me navigate, though thankfully I did have God on my side.

By the end of this book, it is my prayer that you will have all the above. We are going to formulate a battle plan and activate healing for you. In faith, I am trusting and praying on your behalf that you will soon be on the other side of this mountain where you in turn will bring hope and healing to others through your testimony. I see a rich, bright future full of blessing ahead of you. May I *pray* and *prophesy* this over you right now?

PRAYER: Heavenly Father, you see your child right where he or she is right now. At this moment, Father, I stand in the gap for this child of yours and wage war on their behalf. I speak peace into their home, office, car, patio, porch—wherever they are right now. With the power and authority of the name of Jesus, I command the spirit of fear to leave NOW! I commission warring angels to fight and defeat the adversaries who have abused this child of God. I command healing and wholeness in their cognitive functions and calm, blessed assurance in their heart and mind now in Jesus's name.

Heavenly Father, I ask that your messaging and ministering angels assigned to your child bring forward the healing and wholeness purchased by your Son on the day of redemption and restoration. Father, you are altogether holy, all merciful, and wholly good. Breathe your breath into your child's dry bones. May your Holy Spirit awaken this child with the resurrection power of Jesus and bring him/her into the abundant life in Christ Jesus. I ask this of you, our sovereign, almighty Papa God in Jesus's almighty name.

PROPHECY: Precious, redeemed, and restored child of God, I decree and declare that this darkest hour be your greatest victory. You are stronger than you think. You have the resurrection power of Jesus within you. Your giants will be humbled beneath your feet as is your inheritance as joint heir with Jesus (Matthew 22:44). You are destined to do great things to magnify our Savior Jesus and to advance the kingdom of God. Amen and amen!

ACTIVITY K: The Illusion of Control

In the last activity you listed your life battles, which may or may not look like mine. One illusion that can compound anxiety and panic is that we can control every aspect of our lives—and battles. When that illusion of control begins to crumble, so do we —as you've seen in my own story! That said, there are things we can control to some extent, and these can even be part of our coping process. Once again, think about the following questions and jot down all answers that come to mind as comprehensively as possible. For more space, use your journal.

In your specific life battles, describe what you perceive to be within your control.

_____

_____

_____

_____

What is outside of your control?

_____

_____

_____

_____

_____

CHAPTER SEVENTEEN

IMPOSSIBLE THINGS

*"Jesus looked at them and said, 'With man this is
impossible, but with God all things are possible.'"*

MATTHEW 19:26

And yet in all of this I knew that God's ultimate purpose for me
and Scott was to bring healing to our marriage and relationship.
I also knew that this wasn't just about changing my husband but
letting God's Holy Spirit change my own heart and mind and
attitude. One quote from my journal at the time reflects my mulling
over this truth.

> God, not only will you have to change Scott from
> the ground up, you'll have to put new glasses on my
> eyes to see him the way you do.

I also came to understand that moving toward healing in our
relationship wasn't something that would just happen on its own. It
could only begin by taking risks. Faith is trust, and trust takes risks.
I'd taken one small step in giving Scott another chance when he'd
moved back with me and the children. He'd taken a small step in
sharing with me his divine encounter. And I couldn't discount that
ending his relationship and committing to our family was a very big
step on Scott's part, especially considering the emotional mess I'd
become.

But every step–small or large–toward healing still felt unnatural
and risky to the point of being dangerous. It was like the scene
in *Indiana Jones and the Last Crusade* where Harrison Ford must
cross a great chasm to find the Holy Grail. As he reaches the edge
of the chasm, no means of crossing is visible, but to complete his

quest he has to take a leap of faith. In desperation he steps out over the chasm, and just for a moment it looks as though the hero will surely plummet to his death. But as his boot comes down, a narrow footbridge appears miraculously underneath him, camouflaged against the canyon wall. His risky leap of faith results in completing his quest.

The turbulent environment of our home and marriage made every step of trust feel risky and very, very dangerous. But the Holy Spirit kept reminding me it was my heavenly Father who had placed his hand on my back, promising he would lift me high above the circumstances. I had to keep trusting. I had to keep surrendering.

Sometimes I'd feel Jesus ask me, "Even if Scott never esteems you the way you feel he should, am I enough? Is my love enough?"

And despite my pain and panic and grief, I found myself crying out, "Yes, Jesus! You are more than enough for me!"

As I started making an effort to shut down the noise of my emotions and keep my eyes focused on Jesus, I realized I couldn't keep dwelling continuously on a fractured marriage and two broken people. I needed hope. I needed to know that even if those whose position in life should be to love and protect might betray me, God never would (Isaiah 49:15).

Urgently, I began scouring all avenues to find messages of supernatural, abounding hope for hopeless, impossible cases. Of healing for terminally ill marriages. For the authority to proclaim life into dead, decaying hearts and emotions. I found several authors, speakers, and ministers like Katherine Ruonala, Bill Johnson, Leif Hetland, and Joseph Prince, to name a few. I hunted down, seized upon, and devoured every word of hope, every promise of peace, and every dare to dream of joy, purpose, and destiny. I grasped for the lifeline of God's Word, listening to and feeding upon Scripture day and night.

And as I did so, the living Word of God enveloped and held me. I found myself meditating on one psalm in particular, especially as it reads in the original King James Version I'd learned growing up.

He who dwells in the secret place of the Most High
shall abide under the shadow of the Almighty. I will
say of the Lord, "He is my refuge and my fortress;
My God, in him I will trust." (Psalm 91:1-2)

As I pondered this passage, I came to realize several things. It wasn't my husband or any other human in whom I needed to place my trust, but my God, the Almighty, the Most High, my heavenly Father. And when I kept my eyes on Jesus, whose loving eyes were in turn fixed on me as his child, then I was free to dwell in a secret place in Jesus's heart. That secret place of the Most High was my true refuge and fortress.

But healing didn't happen overnight. Nor did it come from some steamy, passionate reconciliation vacation with my husband. Or for that matter, through any therapist or counselor. The greatest pivot points in our healing have been God's handiwork alone, the soft, slow, supernatural transformation effected by the greatest, wisest, most capable, most willing Counselor of all, our heavenly Father, through the work of the Holy Spirit in our lives. Don't get me wrong. I am all for therapists and counselors. But we were so busted no conventional therapist could help.

I remember well another afternoon while walking alone outside around our pool when I began railing out loud. "God, I can't do this! There is no way on earth I can forgive Scott ever. And even if I could forgive him, there's no way I could ever whitewash the memories to unsee them or blot out the pain he's caused. I cannot DO this!"

God answered me immediately: "No, honey, you can't. In and of yourself, you never could. But I can. I have already forgiven Scott, and I will work that forgiveness through you if you'll let me. Just wait and see."

I wasn't accustomed to hearing from God so clearly, but it was unmistakable. Mainly because I knew without a doubt that what I was hearing were not my thoughts. I was thinking thoughts of retaliation. These were thoughts of love, peace, and mercy straight from the Father's heart.

That wasn't the end of it, of course. I bawled and squalled. I raged and shook my fists. But in the end, I consented. I consented to be carried by the one who holds the entire world in his hands. I finally submitted to say as Jesus did to his Father in the Garden of Gethsemane, "Not my will, but yours be done" (Luke 24:42). That is when a transformation began deep within me from loathed to loved, from pain to power, from betrayed to beheld, from abandoned to adored.

This didn't happen overnight, of course. When the temptation came to hold onto the trauma, and feelings of anger and unforgiveness began to smolder, God would intercept with scriptures describing the crucifixion of Jesus. I was reminded that the very people to whom Jesus was sent had rejected him, betrayed him, and crucified him as a common criminal. And yet even as he hung nailed to the cross, Jesus had asked the Father to forgive them "for they don't know what they are doing" (Luke 23:34). If in the face of such rejection and excruciating pain, Jesus could still plead for God's mercy on his betrayers, then I could choose to forgive my husband.

Nor was I the only one experiencing heart transformation. While I was focused on my own need for healing and search for answers, God was working a transformation in my husband as well—even when I wasn't seeing it or particularly cared to. Jesus had really captured Scott in that divine encounter, and like the metamorphosis going on within the hard chrysalis of a butterfly, God was breaking down the hard shell he'd acquired along the way to protect himself, releasing the beautiful man of God, husband, and father God had designed him to be. That's our Father. That's our Savior. Oh, the many wonders of his love!

Practical Help for PTSD and Anxiety Disorder

Before we go any further, if you are suffering or recovering from PTSD or anxiety disorder, I just want to spend a few moments with you right here. The most important thing I want to say to you right now is *this is not your new normal.* These symptoms are NOT going to last forever. Your mind and body will return to a calm state. I promise you it will!

But until those calm feelings materialize, let me share a few battle tactics I've learned in walking through the trauma of anxiety disorder. Remember in our last activity we looked at what things we can control to some extent as well as those we can't. And I mentioned then that utilizing what we can control can become useful strategies to help us cope. You may already have listed some. But below are a few that have worked for me. Feel free to borrow these while you come up with your own list. Hopefully one or more of these will be helpful to you right away.

1. If you can, seek help from a therapist who has experience with PTSD. Have them teach you some practical coping strategies for staving off panic attacks. There are any number that can help. A good therapist can also help with sorting through your trauma and expedite healing from it.

2. Stay in the present. Do not look out into the future. And as much as you possibly can, try not to study the past. When those scenes and images of a traumatic event come across your memory screen, take a deep breath, switch gears, and move your thoughts back into the present.

3. Use your phone's calendar function to set reminders. For me, I thought I could and would remember little events and activities throughout the week. I've always been able to before. But I just couldn't. Finally, after missing multiple activities and commitments, I stared using my phone's calendar. I did try notes and lists, but that only lasted as long as I knew where that slippery little notepad was. Even today, if it isn't on my phone's calendar, it doesn't get done.

4. Prioritize what absolutely must get done in the next hour or two. If it's overwhelming to you, don't even try to process and prioritize the whole day's activities and responsibilities. Don't put more on your plate than you absolutely must for the

moment. If you're getting through lunchtime and you can't deal with dinner plans, then DON'T! Frozen dinners, take-out, order-in, whatever works is the right call. Remember, this is not forever, just for right now.

5.   At work, talk to your boss or someone in HR (Human Resources) who can help you reduce your responsibilities for a time. You can explain your situation without giving details. If you can, take a few days off or more if possible.

6.   Spend time if possible with a supportive friend or family member who will listen without judgment or asking a ton of questions. Talk if you can. Your loved ones and friends may not understand exactly what you are going through right now, but they do love you and want the very best for you. As much as you can, don't punish them by removing yourself, your time, or affection from them. Just being with loved ones will help you heal faster.

7.   As best you can, try not to isolate yourself. It delays healing.

8.   If you are having full-blown panic attacks, get your doctor to prescribe you appropriate medication you can take as needed. I'm serious! NO ONE should have to endure panic attacks without some help. Only people who have never had a panic attack would ever criticize you for it. God created intelligence, doctors, and the science behind medication, so don't let anyone make you feel guilty about availing yourself. We will of course give Jesus all the glory, not if but WHEN your healing and liberty from PTSD/anxiety manifests.

9.   If you are struggling with throat symptoms like feeling a lump or scratchiness or tightness, keep a super-strong mint or lozenge such as Altoid's or Fisherman's Friend in your wallet, handbag, vehicle, desk, nightstand, and everywhere else you frequent. That strong sort of burning flavor helped me many times a day to breathe deeply, stay present in the moment, and not get sucked up into the whirling winds of panic.

10. Lastly, when guilt and condemnation come—and they will—shelve them. You're going to make some mistakes. We all do every day, never mind during terribly stressful times in our lives. Your brain isn't processing at peak performance right now. Decision-making and problem-solving are evasive at best. Give yourself grace. You are well on your way to being whole again.

CHAPTER EIGHTEEN

HEALING

"For I am about to do something new. See, I have already
begun! Do you not see it? I will make a pathway through the
wilderness. I will create rivers in the dry wasteland."

ISAIAH 43:19, NLT

I can pinpoint the exact pivotal event in our lives when our marriage as well as our personal healing reached a turning point—January 2018.

Healing had been taking place all along, of course, over the past almost three years. But it was so gradual that only looking back over a span of many months could I really see a distinct change. My panic attacks hadn't gone away, but as I focused my eyes on Jesus, they became fewer and less intense. Instead of finding a home for me and the kids and a separate apartment for Scott, as had been our original plan, we purchased a nice home to share. Beyond being together as a family, this turned out to be an added blessing as with my panic attacks I simply couldn't hold a job.

Meanwhile as we plugged into our new local church and immersed ourselves in solid Bible teaching, Scott was also growing spiritually. The more he discovered God's unconditional love for him, the more he understood his own identity in Christ, the more he trusted God with his whole heart. I could see him opening up like a tight flower bud unfurling. With his mom gone, we were all he had left as immediate family, and he began investing more time and emotion into his children as well as into our own relationship. Slowly, he was becoming less defensive with me, kinder, more patient, and more wise in ways of the Lord. We were both praying individually and with our children at night, but slowly, tentatively, we began coming together to pray as a couple.

That didn't mean it became easier. We were still sniping at each other. Criticizing the other's shortcomings instead of complements or kind words was an old habit and hard to break. To like each other again, enjoy each other's company, much less love each other sometimes seemed an impossible goal.

Then everything changed. Not the slow, gradual crawl that healing had been to this point, but an instantaneous supernatural transformation. For some time, I'd been wanting to learn more about God's calling on my life in healing, as my mother had prophesied since my childhood as well as the revival evangelist when I was fourteen. I'd researched the School of Supernatural Healing taught by Randy Clark at Bethel Church in Redding, CA, and felt strongly that God was directing me to attend their three-day conference in January.

Scott and I did some planning that would allow me to fly to California while he worked from home to care for our children in my absence. But when I attempted to book a registration online, just a few clicks informed me that the event was sold out. I was crushed. I emailed Bethel, the hosting church, asking if there was any way I could still get a ticket. I quickly received a kind response apologizing that the event was indeed sold out.

"Okay, Lord, I really thought that was your directive," I prayed. "But you will do it your way, and I will be good with whatever you choose."

Just then I sensed the Holy Spirit prompting my heart, "Make Scott a cup of coffee." I'd already made a pot of coffee and had actually been about to ask Scott if he wanted one. But I again sensed the Holy Spirit instructing, "No, **make** Scott a cup of coffee."

Without any real enthusiasm, I went over to the coffee pot, prepared a cup of coffee just the way Scott likes it, then carried it over to him. Scott looked surprised and pleased at my unsolicited—and unusual—act of service.

"Oh, wow! Thank you!" he said, taking the cup.

Not five seconds later, my phone rang. It was Bethel. They'd just found a few more available seats. Would I still like to attend?

Those three days at Bethel changed my life. I had expected to learn more about how to operate more confidently in healing others. But God had other plans. He wanted to heal me. Friday afternoon's sessions especially with Randy Clark were a call to action. He asked us, "Will you let the Lord use you in the way he wants to use you? Will you completely yield yourself?"

When I responded to the call, Randy prayed over me. I felt the Holy Spirit fire rise up in me from my stomach to my head, not in any gentle caress but so that it seemed I was roasting with such intensity I could barely endure the heat. I also felt in a way I'd never imagined just how deeply I was loved by my heavenly Father. From that moment, God delivered me instantaneously and miraculously from my anxiety, the panic attacks, my desire to smoke and drink, even my dysfunctional thyroid and high blood pressure. And just as with my bone tumor when I was ten, I *knew* I'd been healed even before I tested it all out.

When I arrived back home, I had a difficult time explaining to Scott what had transpired. In truth, I didn't understand it all myself. After sharing my experience as much as I could describe, I said to him, "I don't know what's going to change, but I'm sure something is, and I can't wait to see what is in store."

The most obvious change was the abrupt end of my craving to smoke and drink. The smoking was immediate even while I was still at the conference. For a long time, I had medicated with alcohol to banish pain. I still experienced a fleeting desire, but now I could say to myself, "You don't want that anymore. It doesn't taste as good as you think, and the freedom from it is far more delicious than giving in."

With neither Scott nor I drinking anymore, our relationship changed drastically as well. For one, I was much less emotional. We started with baby steps immediately after my trip, looking for kind and complimentary things to say to each other instead of criticizing. One pivotal moment was when Scott was doing the dishes and I suddenly realized I *loved* the way he filled the dishwasher— so precisely and neatly, the spoons all facing the same way, dishes lined up with military precision, completely different from my own haphazard method. When I told him how much I liked the way he did it, I received in response a big, spontaneous smile. That in itself was a miracle!

Later on for the first time in what seemed an eternity, Scott looked at me appreciatively and said, "You look beautiful today, Ami."

One kind and loving expression of words led to another. I'd been so furious for so long I hadn't wanted to compliment Scott on what a good-looking man he was because I didn't want him thinking too highly of himself. Above all, thinking of how attractive he was to women. As I released that fear and expressed my appreciation openly, he responded in kind. Just finding something lighthearted and humorous to say to each other instead of always being serious or angry became one of our great pivotal points of healing.

I had once told God in my journal that he'd not only have to change Scott but put new glasses on my eyes so I could see him as God did. And God had done just that. As Scott and I began valuing each other's positive characteristics and natures we possessed all along instead of seeing only the negative, we were seeing each other through a different pair of glasses. Through God's glasses.

ACTIVITY L: Your Choice

Bottom line, as I hope you've seen by now, we can't control our lives or destiny on our own—much less win our own battles. What we do control is who *does* control our lives and destiny. That choice will determine the outcome of our battles—and the formulation of our battle plan. Once again, think about and answer the following questions as comprehensively as possible. For more space, use your journal.

Who do you perceive as being in control of your life? Why?

_____

_____

_____

If you haven't asked God to place your life and destiny under his control, then do so now. Write that request here and include the date for a permanent record of your choice.

_____

_____

_____

Have you formulated a battle plan to date? If so, what is it?

_____

_____

CHAPTER NINETEEN

TRANSFORMATION

"Here am I and the children whom the LORD has
given me! We are for signs and wonders in Israel from
the Lord of hosts, who dwells in Mount Zion."

ISAIAH 8:18, NKJV

I haven't experienced a single panic attack since returning from Bethel. The simple relief of awakening each morning without a sense of overwhelming doom has been huge. Believe me, the devil has tried very hard to bring them back, and I've still faced some feelings of overwhelming dread from day to day. But instead of letting them sweep me away, I breathe through it, reminding myself, "You have been healed by God. There is nothing wrong with you."

Nor did Scott and I create the perfect marriage overnight. We still had arguments. We still relapsed into old patterns of hurting each other. But we were growing and learning to both apologize and forgive. And the deliverance from alcohol dependency, once such a big part of our relationship, made a huge difference.

More than once over the years after a heated argument, Scott had simply jumped into his car and driven off. One day during this period, Guy witnessed us arguing and his father taking off. I phoned Scott, catching up with him a few minutes down the road.

"Your son saw you," I told him. "He's afraid you're going to leave and never come back."

Scott turned around and drove home. Guy was standing there with a tearstained face, looking so much like Scott had at the same age. The stark reminder of how Scott's own father had abandoned him as a child and never returned broke Scott's heart. Hugging Guy, he assured him fervently, "I'll never leave you again."

We both came to see that Scott's impulse to run when our marriage got ugly was similar to my own panic attacks. And like me, with God's help he could learn to resist it. He has kept his word, and a threat of leaving when things get hard is no longer an option for either of us.

There have also been times when I relapse into the false teaching of my childhood that somehow I have to be good enough to earn God's favor and that if I don't constantly strive and achieve, I will flunk out as a mother, wife, and Christian. But I've learned to listen to my heavenly Father's loving assurance that just as I can do nothing on my own to earn merit with God, so nothing I fail to achieve is going to cause me to "flunk out." I am a child of God. Whatever God may permit me to do in his service is not so I can pass the course, but more like "extra credit."

"Ami, I've got you," my heavenly Father assured me. "I am the lifter of your head (Psalm 3:3), and I will not let you fall. You aren't going to fail the course. With my strength and power, you are going to save your marriage and family from generational abuse, abandonment, and brokenness. You are going to build a family that stays together even when there has been treacherous wrongdoing. You are going to raise your children as World-Changers who are steadfast, resilient, and strong. Who base their perspective on me and who I am to them and who they are in me."

I would never have dreamed in January 2018 where God would bring our family today. It's like when bread rises, and where there was only a small puddle of dough at the bottom of a bread pan, in just a few hours it grows into a full loaf overflowing the pan. At Bethel, I'd asked God to give me a passion after his heart to do whatever he asks. Since my return, God began putting me in the path of other people to whom I could minister and pray for them. I started serving in women's ministry and prayer ministry at our church and began an inspirational blog.

I also started working with two other ladies in a ministry of spiritual empowerment, which has included weekly ministry, Bible study, discipleship, and training teachers. Recently, I began an inner and physical healing group in our church. Scott and I began homeschooling our kids, who were in first and third grade.

Then God brought a new adventure into our home. Our church has a major ministry emphasis on fostering with the church providing a supporting team for each foster family within the church. God laid this ministry in a special way on Scott's heart. We did our paperwork to become foster parents and were finally approved. In October 2018, a four-month-old baby who had been rescued from human trafficking was placed with us. In September 2019, we finished the adoption process, and we officially became a family of five.

Scott and I also started our own home-based software consulting business called 1Group Consulting. Scott had been sharing with me his own vision for the future that he'd been praying about with God. Then God laid on his heart to dream and build bigger than anything he'd had audacity to do so far in his life. He'd always excelled in mentoring others in the implementation of software projects and managing the development of new systems for businesses, so in essence he was already working as a consultant.

The business allows us both to work together from home. I handle the marketing while Scott does the consulting and business travel. Which in turn allows Scott to be closely involved in our children's activities and in ministry together as a couple in our church.

By this point I considered my life more than full and busy. But God wasn't done. In the summer of 2018, he spoke to me with the message he'd once given Moses about the Israelites who were slaves in Egypt (Exodus 3).

"Set my captives free!" I heard clearly.

"What do you want me to do, Lord?" I asked.

And just as he'd once asked Moses (Exodus 4:2), he said to me, "What is that in your hand, Ami?"

I didn't think I had anything in my hand except a basket full of past fears, disappointment, failure, and pain. When I pointed this out to God, he said, "Through me, you have been given the power and tools to overcome these. Now you need to share this with other captives."

That is when I began writing this book.

CHAPTER TWENTY

FEAR NOT!

*"Peace I leave with you; my peace I give you. I do
not give to you as the world gives. Do not let your
hearts be troubled and do not be afraid."*

JOHN 14:27

Going back to the core theme of this book and the wonderful
truth that transformed my own fear-dominated life. We don't
have to live with fear, depression, or anxiety in any capacity. In fact,
we MUST NOT live with it. It's from the enemy! Fear is the enemy's
chief contaminating weapon used to poison our peace and joy and
the fullness of our potential that God himself ordained and provided
through his Son Jesus Christ. Fear is the evidence of lost trust and
inaccurate identity. Few of us are unscathed by its toxic touch.

Left unchecked, this type of "left-over" fear finds a chink in our
belief-system armor and corrodes until a hole appears. That hole
soon becomes large enough for a spirit of fear to invite itself in. Once
inside our armor, the enemy continues to leverage fear to enlarge
the hole from the inside. Then he invites more of his friends to join
him like bitterness, anger, and hatred. Before long, we are walking
around with the weightiness of all these characteristics inside us.
We are not our authentic, God-created, Jesus-purchased, redeemed,
and restored selves.

Little by little the toxins of emotional injury and trauma leech
into the thirsty soil of our souls and contaminate the roots. The
byproducts are evident in the spindly hope for our future, sparse
peace, stunted wisdom, and near-extinct joy. Fear backs us into a
corner and squashes our hope, peace, and identity.

Vanquishing Satan's Myths and Misconception

So what should be our response? We've got to punch back! We must back fear into its own corner and keep it there. I'm talking TKO—Total Knock Out. If we allow fear to remain standing, we will not reach our full potential of who God has called and created us to be.

Worse still, we do not perceive and receive all that Jesus died for and made available to us as our inheritance. We talked earlier (in chapter five) about how the chastisement, the payment, for our peace was purchased by our Savior (Isaiah 53:5). That too is part of our inheritance as children of God and co-heirs with Jesus. Are you at peace today? Are you able to sit at the feet of Jesus and allow him who always was, who is, and who is to come, the Word who became flesh and dwelt among us, to minister to you and bring you into peace?

If your answer is no, I have good news to share! You are in the right place right now to allow the Prince of Peace to minister to you. Let's see what Jesus himself has to say about it.

> Come to me all who are weary and burdened, and I will give you rest. Take my yoke upon you and learn from me, for I am gentle and humble in heart, and you will find rest for your souls. For my yoke is easy and my burden is light. (Matthew 11:28-30)

Notice that the word *rest* is mentioned two times. By repeating the word, Jesus is emphasizing and establishing the truth regarding how we obtain peace. The image here is removing a heavy, burdensome, wearying yoke we've shouldered ourselves or allowed someone to place on us and replacing it with the easy, light load that is Jesus's yoke. That doesn't happen automatically. We have to "take" Jesus's yoke and rest it upon our shoulders.

That takes deliberate choice and repeated practice. I know some folks who practice yoga and swear by it. I'd like you and I instead to practice "yoke-a." Okay, that may sound a bit corny, but it's an illustration of an intentional practice of unshouldering burdens that don't come from Jesus and taking on only what does come from him.

How do we know which burdens are from us/others and which are from Jesus? I'm glad you asked. A full answer could be another entire book in and of itself. But the short answer is this. If it causes stress, fear, or anxiety, it's probably not from the Lord. If it brings peace, fulfillment, and joy, you can just bet that's from the Lord.

Let me add a caveat here. There are times when God asks us to do things like reconciling broken relationships or forgiving and loving those who have hated or hurt us. These can feel very uncomfortable and even painful in our human nature. And troubles come. I'd say most of us are walking through one type of adverse circumstance or another right now. In fact, Jesus himself gives us a heads up on that count.

> I [Jesus] have told you these things, so that in me you may have peace. In this world you will have trouble. But take heart! I have overcome the world. (John 16:33)

Notice that peace isn't the result of having no troubles. Peace is being with Jesus. Our loving, gentle, humble, kind Savior has overcome the troubles we will encounter in this world, and the burden he asks us to carry is easy and light enough so that we can be at rest. But that again means coming to Jesus and taking on his yoke in place of our weary, burdensome one. That includes releasing our stress, fear, and anxiety to him. In my experience, that is a practical definition for being at peace.

So then, peace is not defined as the absence of fear. Rather, peace is reconciling fear to the cross. There is a divine exchange that happens here. We take our fear, our dis-order, our un-rest and exchange it for Jesus's purchased peace and rest. I use mental imagery in doing so— taking the burden of fear and anxiety off my own head and shoulders and placing it on Jesus's scourged shoulders and back where the chastisement for our peace was paid in full. In its place, I mentally take up Jesus's easy, light, restful yoke and place that on my own shoulders.

I do self-checks on my peace status frequently, sometimes several times a day. I highly recommend this. When the noise-level of fear, chaos, or stress is amplified and shouting louder than peace, it's time to take action. It's time to practice the "yoke-a." You got it!

Now What?

President Franklin D. Roosevelt, who gave leadership to the American nation during WW2, is famously quoted as saying, "We have nothing to fear but fear itself."

Now I have great admiration and respect for FDR, but I must humbly disagree with his statement. As children of God, we don't need to fear even fear itself! (We do need to fear God, but we've already talked about what a different kind of fear that is.) Fearing fear and/or avoiding fear are equally red flags. And avoidance is not a battle plan. To defeat our enemy, we must face our enemy. That means facing our fears.

I hope by now you have a pretty solid idea of where your fears came from and why they exist. This is important to know as we move on to the main purpose for all we've been walking through these last twenty chapters and what I promised when we started this journey—i.e., to share how we can become **more-than-conquerors** in our battle against the spirit of fear. We can't change the past. But praise God, we can reshape and redirect the present so as to achieve God's purpose and destiny for our future. Now that we know our true identity, purpose, and inheritance as children of God, it is time to strategize an effective battle plan to defeat fear and keep it defeated forever.

We Don't Fight Alone

There is one other important truth to keep in mind as we formulate our battle plan. You may already be saying, "Whoa!! I can't go into battle against the enemy. I can't fight the spirit of fear. I'm just not strong enough, brave enough, powerful enough."

The good news is that you don't have to. We aren't more than conquerors on our own. We are more than conquerors because God is for us (Romans 8:31, 37). We have on our side Abba, Father God, the Creator of all, who is Love and who loves us profoundly. We have our Lord and Savior Jesus Christ, whose stripes paid for our peace and who is now seated at the right hand of the Father making intercession on our behalf. We have our Helper and Advocate the Holy Spirit who teaches us all things and also intercedes for us. We have heavenly hosts of ministering, messaging, commissioning, warring, and protecting angels assigned to watch over us (Psalm 91:11-12, Matthew 18:10, Hebrews 1:14).

And we have each other, our brothers and sisters in the family of God, designed by God to be one body (1 Corinthians 12:12-27) to care for each other, suffer together, rejoice together—and battle together. Jesus himself promised that when his church is on the march, the gates of hell itself can't stand against us (Matthew 16:17). That means we are not going into battle alone, but with powerful allies.

So now that we are ready, here is our battle plan for conquering that spirit of fear in our lives. Over these final chapters, we will take a look at each strategy individually and how they build on each other to give us the victory.

Battle Plan for Defeating Fear

- Know your attacker and his strategies
- Stand and face the giant
- Slay the giant
- Abide, rest
- Partner and participate with the Holy Spirit
- Safeguard your peace
- Fix your eyes on Jesus

CHAPTER TWENTY-ONE

KNOW THE ENEMY

> *"Now the serpent was more crafty than any of the wild animals the Lord God had made. He said to the woman, 'Did God really say you must not eat from any tree in the garden? You will not certainly die, for God knows that when you eat from it your eyes will be opened, and you will be like God, knowing good from evil.'"*

GENESIS 31:1, 4-5

Battle Strategy #1: Know Your Attacker and His Strategies

In creating an effective battle strategy, the first step is to understand just who our enemy is and what his battle strategy is against us. The enemy's goal is to steal, kill, and destroy (John 10:10). He will make every attempt to steal the promises we have received from the Lord, to kill our identity as a child of God, and to destroy the peace and joy Jesus has granted us.

So how does he do that? Let's take a look at just a few of the battle strategies Satan uses that you may even recognize as having been effective in your own life.

Distractions: We often fall for distractions when the demand for our attention is high. For example, a friend or family member encounters difficulty and we let ourselves be drawn or pulled into the situation beyond what is healthy. Or a project at work is under intense pressure and we throw ourselves in full tilt beyond what is sustainable. Or we get distracted by things happening around us like current events or daily news.

Another distraction is comparison shopping through social media. Facebook, Twitter, Instagram, and other social media invites us to compare ourselves to others. We can spend hours on social media comparing ourselves, our socio-economic status, jobs, houses, relationships, marriages, spouses, children, dogs, cats to other people's. Comparison is tremendously disruptive and a breeding ground for insecurity. We don't need that!

I am on social media, but I try diligently to just get my updates submitted and not shop around. I will admit I sometimes fail in this objective. I start looking for an old classmate or college buddy, and by the time I've finished, I've spent forty-five precious minutes of my time. Even worse, I come away feeling a little less secure, a little less than the apple of God's eye.

Does that sound familiar? Okay, let's pinky-promise not to let social media (read in "comparison invitation") be our go-to time-filler or hobby. It is not a good use of our time or emotions. Instead, subscribe to daily devotionals and a few inspirational bloggers or speakers. Before you know it, you won't have the time or desire to spend on social media.

News and social media are certainly not the only peace saboteurs that barrage us daily. There are so many like the rude person who steals our parking spot or cuts us off. Not to mention the countless distractions that happen at home. We still have to manage and resolve many of the distractions. The goal is to not get derailed by them. Come back to the awareness of God's presence. Come back to God's Word. Come back to the objective of peace.

Pain, disappointments, trauma: Now some of this is unavoidable. People have done mean, horrible things to us that have scarred us for life. And some pain we've brought on ourselves. Regardless of how it happened, it's crucial that we not hold onto the pain. Pain digs pits. Absolutely, there's a time to grieve. But then we need to make a decision. We can stay wallowing in the pit of pain or allow healing to begin.

Make the decision during your journey through this book to allow healing to begin. Read the sections on identity, purpose, and inheritance over and over again until it sinks in who you are, Whose you are, and Who your Healer is. Life is too short and your purpose and destiny is too incredible to stay stuck in the pit.

Shame: I've done things in my life I'm terribly ashamed of. Things so shameful and abhorrent that I've grieved those decisions and resulting consequences. As with Adam and Eve, shame tells us we're not worthy. That we should never ask to come back into the Father's arms. But shame is a scam. And our heavenly Father has never released us from his arms even when we've turned our faces away to behold shame instead of his loving kindness. Let's not be scammed any longer.

Isolation: This tool of the devil is a formidable battle strategy. If the enemy can get us off on our own little island of struggle and make us believe we're all alone, we are easy pickings. Sitting ducks. Here's the truth. Every single struggle you're walking through, someone else is too. And others have not only walked through that same struggle but are now on the other side proclaiming victory in the name of Jesus. If you don't have people available who will pray for you, submit your prayer request to our ministry at *prayer@greaterthingstoday. com*. We'd be honored to pray with you and for you.

Discouragement: Have you ever set out on a road trip with a projected ETA (estimated time of arrival) only to be challenged with roadwork, an accidental wrong turn, and heavy traffic? Now your ETA is blown, and you have no idea when or even if you'll ever arrive. The devil loves when we become discouraged and will throw every roadblock he can in our path to delay us and keep us from believing we'll ever arrive to our destination. But he is a liar.

Unforgiveness: Similar to pain, disappointment, and trauma, we are ultimately in control of the effects of unforgiveness on our lives. Unforgiveness is a ball-and-chain shackled to our ankles, and we hold the key to freedom in our own hands. The enemy doesn't want us to walk free, so he keeps dropping bread crumb reminders and whispers of pain. He continuously feeds our anger to keep the coals of unforgiveness alive.

I've already shared my own tipping point in forgiveness that day outside by our pool and the resulting heart transformation in both

Scott and me. But it begins with making a choice, not necessarily to forgive, but to be willing to be made willing to forgive. Once we have submitted our will to God to be made willing to forgive, it is God who works within us the will and the ability/power to do things for his good purpose (Philippians 2:13), which includes working his forgiveness in our hearts.

Bitterness: Bitterness is anger, hurt, disappointment, and unforgiveness with a spirit root attached to it. It must be pulled up by the root, rebuked, and cast out forever. It's as simple as that. Otherwise, it grows inside us, contaminating as it grows, poisoning our perspective of identity, inheritance, and purpose. It must be eradicated. We will do this together in the Activating Healing chapter. But if you want to get a head-start, go for it!

Fear: I've heard fear defined as the following acronym: False Evidence Appearing Real. Fear is a counterfeit emotion and too frequently has a spirit root attached to it. It is not part of our identity, purpose, or inheritance in Christ, and must be evicted.

Once you become aware that fear, discouragement, bitterness, unforgiveness, depression, anxiety, etc. are lies and deceit of the devil, you are well on your way to victory. You are not alone in having to face such attacks. Satan taunted Jesus over and over during his forty-day fast in the wilderness (Matthew 4:1-11, Mark 1:12-13, Luke 4:1-13).

The devil knew Jesus's weakened state, and that's when Old Scratch started troubling and testing Jesus. That's exactly what happens to us too. The devil will come to test us when we are weak, tired, frustrated, hurt and/or distracted. Why? That's when we are most vulnerable. The devil fights dirty!! He's a roaring, devouring lion, slinking and sneaking up on unsuspecting, unaware victims.

The good news is that Jesus gave us by example our weapon in battling the devil's temptations—God's Word (Hebrews 4:12-13). We've mentioned that before and will discuss it more when we talk about slaying our giants.

ACTIVITY M: Choosing to Forgive

As we've stated several times, forgiveness is a choice. It begins first with letting God change your heart so that you are even willing to make that choice. Let's do that now together. Take the key to that ball-and-chain shackle of unforgiveness in your hand and hold it firmly. Then pray with me: "Father, I am willing to be made willing to forgive. I thank you that you work within me both the willingness and the grace to do it for the glory of Jesus. Amen."

Okay, the key has turned and the shackles have fallen away, leaving you free to forgive. Now let's avail ourselves of that freedom. Think of the person you need to forgive and what that person has done to you that needs forgiven. Write below your own prayer of forgiveness along the following general parameters:

"Heavenly Father, thank you for making me willing to forgive (so-and-so) for (such-and-such). I choose today (include date) to forgive (so-and-so) for (such-and-such). I choose to continue forgiving from this date forward and to act with forgiveness regardless of my emotions. Please continue to work in my heart to help me feel emotionally the mental and spiritual choice I've made to forgive (so-and-so).

_____

_____

_____

_____

Each time you find yourself wrestling again with forgiveness, come back here to reread your commitment. Repeat this process if you have multiple people you need to forgive. For more space, use your journal.

CHAPTER TWENTY-TWO

FACE THE ENEMY

"Who is this uncircumcised Philistine that he should defy the armies of the living God?"

1 SAMUEL 17:26

Battle Strategy #2: Stand and Face Your Giants

Which brings us to our next battle strategy—taking our stand against the enemy. I mentioned earlier that avoidance is not a battle plan. Scripture gives us an excellent example of this. Maybe you remember from Sunday school as a child the exciting tale of the shepherd boy David defeating the colossal giant Goliath who was threatening the nation of Israel (1 Samuel 17). That story isn't just for little children. It is an applicable warfare lesson for us today.

Just a few details to keep in mind if you don't remember the whole story (and may I encourage you to read the entire chapter in the Bible). David was the youngest of seven brothers, and his earthly father didn't have big plans for him, sending him off to tend sheep while David's other brothers occupied more important roles. But God had king-sized plans for David. God taught David to rely on God's power to slay lions and bears that had attacked his sheep.

David also practiced God's presence out there alone with his flocks, worshipping God and singing praises to God. In all that time together, God was teaching David who David was, shaping David's identity as a son of God and future king of Israel. So by the time David faced Goliath, he was sure of his identity. Now that is the battle-winning secret!

Just who was this giant? The Bible says that Goliath was massive in stature, skilled in battle, and the most powerful weapon Israel's enemies possessed at the time. He was also highly skilled in emotional propaganda, loudly insulting, antagonizing, and intimidating. He was taunting Israel's army, challenging them to take him on in single combat. When David showed up, Goliath ridiculed the idea that a mere boy without armor or sword could challenge him.

We can expect this behavior from Goliath since he was the enemy and his objective was to intimidate and humiliate. What is more surprising is how David's own brothers mocked and shamed him. David had originally arrived at the battlefield to bring his older brothers food to eat as per their father's instruction. But rather than cheering him on, they ridiculed him and told him to get back to his sheep (1 Samuel 17:28).

INTIMIDATION

Say it out loud: "Intimidation!" The devil will use whomever and whatever means he can to intimidate you when you step up to fight for your God-given, Jesus-paid identity and inheritance. When you are fighting for peace, you can expect that people you've counted as your best friends all your life, possibly even your own family, may not understand. Many might desert you. But you are NOT alone, not by a long shot! You are NEVER alone!

How did David respond? First, he refused the loan of King Saul's armor, making a conscious decision to be his authentic self, clothed solely in the armor of his experiential knowledge of the Lord. He then decreed victory, yelling right back at Goliath's insults and taunts that his God would deliver Goliath over to him. David was not intimidated. On the contrary, he was crazy-bold and confident.

Why? Because David had history with the Lord. He knew Abba's voice. Over and over God had proven himself faithful in impossible circumstances like the lion and the bear. David knew God was on his side in this battle as well and had full confidence Father God would deliver the giant over to him because God always had. In the end, David used the enemy's own sword to strike the fatal blow. Irony in the Bible—awesome!

The Bible passage tells us that David stepped into the greatest fight of his life with nothing more than the rudimentary, inferior weapon of a shepherd boy—a sling and five smooth stones. But did you know the number five in Hebrew represents grace? That is significant because it is only by God's grace that we have the power through His Spirit to defeat the enemy of fear.

And why would God grace us with His Spirit and power? He wants us to win!! He wants us to take our positions and place as his sons and daughters, to bring glory to the Son and fulfill the redemption plan of Jesus's holy, more than sufficient sacrifice. Your adoring Papa also wants you to fulfill the plans he dreamed and planned for you at the foundations of creation.

Once he became king, David waged war against his adversaries continuously throughout his reign. But God was for him, and he won the battles. David loved God with all his heart. Even so, David made terrible choices and horrible mistakes, including adultery and murder (2 Samuel 11). Does that remind you of anyone you know? I can certainly see myself in his mistakes!

But David also repented profoundly, and God forgave him, restoring him to prosperity, protection, and honor (2 Samuel 12). God called David "a man after my own heart" (1 Samuel 13:14, Acts 13:22). When David's son Solomon became king, Solomon declared to the people of Israel:

> You know that my father, David, was not able to build a Temple to honor the name of the LORD his God because of the many wars waged against him by surrounding nations. He could not build until the LORD gave him victory over all his enemies. But now the LORD my God has given me peace on every side; I have no enemies, and all is well. (1 Kings 3-4, NLT)

FACING YOUR GIANT

"What does this have to do with me?" you may be asking. "I'm no warrior like David. I can't even shoot a sling shot!"

It has everything to do with you, so just listen, powerful and powerfully loved child of God, because the next few statements are critical. First, you've already won the battle because you are in Christ. Remember your inheritance as co-heir with Jesus (and if you don't remember, go back and re-read that section). The game is totally fixed. The score is already on the board. Sickness, death, the enemy, and all his tactics and minions are under Jesus's feet. You are seated in heavenly places with Christ, who is ruling in victory. Therefore, you enjoy the spoils of his victory. As Jesus is in heaven, so are you on this earth—ruling and governing all things that have already been placed under Jesus's feet.

There is just one thing standing in your way—a leering, taunting, lying enemy. You are going to make a decision and a promise to God and to yourself that together with him you will stand and face the giant. Don't turn your back on fear. Face your enemy until it flees. Be courageous. If you can't do it without fear, then do it afraid. Courage isn't the lack of fear. It's standing in the face of fear. Remember what the apostle Paul had to say about putting on our spiritual armor:

> Finally, be strong in the Lord and in his mighty power. Put on the full armor of God, so that you can **take your stand** against the devil's schemes. For our struggle is not against flesh and blood, but against the rulers, against the authorities, against the powers of this dark world and against the spiritual forces of evil in the heavenly realms. Therefore put on the full armor of God, so that when the day of evil comes, you may be able to **stand your ground**, and **after you have done everything, to stand. Stand firm** then . . . (Ephesians 6:10-14)

Do you see how many times we are told to STAND in that passage? And where does our strength and power come from to be able to stand? It comes from God. We can't face our giants alone. But we CAN do it together with him. And what happens when we take our stand armored in God's armor and strengthened by God's power? The apostle James tells us that.

> Submit yourselves, then, to God. Resist the devil,
> and he will flee from you. (James 4:7)

That's right! When you submit yourself first to God so that you are facing the enemy with God's strength and power, the devil doesn't stand a chance. So stand that liar down in Jesus's name! You'll find that the enemy is no giant at all. His large, loud stature and intimidation are all smoke and mirrors. Just stand!

Now this means remaining laser-focused until you have the victory. Don't walk away from this fight until fear is under your feet. Lift Jesus up over this situation and apply his victorious blood to it. How do I implement this practically in my daily life?

First, I start my day praying something like this: "Jesus, I thank you that your blood encircles me, my husband and my children individually and this family collectively. You are a hedge of protection (Psalms 91) and a wall of fire all around me (Zechariah 2:25)."

Then throughout the day, I will repeat, "There is a Jesus Christ blood-line encircling my mind and heart; I have the mind of Christ."

I also sing songs of worship. I enter into the secret place in Psalms 91 (see more about this later). I envision myself on the mercy seat of the Ark of the Covenant between the wings of the two cherubim with God's grace and mercy pouring out upon me.

Lastly, I get back up on my feet every time I fall down. The reality is that we're going to slip and fall at times. Maybe you're dealing with substance abuse, eating disorders, pornography, or other addictions, and you find yourself falling back into old patterns. But when (not if) we fall, we need to fall forward, not backward. We fall into our identity as sons and daughter of God. Then we need to get back up on our feet and take our stand. Even when none of this makes sense anymore, when no one around you supports your decisions, when you're tired of the battle and you want to give up, just HOLD ON and cling to our Savior's beautiful promise for the weary warrior.

> Peace I leave with you; my peace I give to you. Not as the world gives do I give to you. Let not your hearts be troubled, neither let them be afraid. (John 14:27, ESV)

You are going to formulate your own strategy. But in the meantime, feel free to use mine. I promise you, fear will soon be under your feet, and Jesus will be magnified as you take your rightful position as joint-heirs with him.

Crushing Fear

One thing to keep in mind as you stand your ground is that our enemy likes to launch his fiery darts when we are tired. That's a number one strategy for the devil. But he also likes to sneak-attack when we've gotten accustomed to victory and have let our guard down. Make it a practice every day to draw a Jesus Christ blood-line of protection around you. Memorize some fear-crushing scripture verses that you can speak over yourself out loud daily. Meditate on one promise per week until it becomes second nature to you. Keep meditating on it until it becomes your first nature. Then meditate even more until it becomes your true identity and no circumstance can shake it. Here are some of my favorites.

> I have the mind of Christ. (Philippians 2:5-8)

> He has not given me a spirit of fear; He has given me the Spirit of power of love and a sound mind. (2 Timothy 1:7)

Greater is He who is in me than he who is in the world. (1 John 4:4)

I shall not die but live and declare the glorious works of the Lord. (Psalms 118:17)

God loves me with an everlasting love. (Jeremiah 31:3)

There is no fear in love. But perfect love drives out fear because fear has to do with punishment. The one who fears is not made perfect in love. (1 John 4:18)

The Darkest Hour is Just Before Dawn

Before we move on from the David and Goliath story, I want to take a moment to point out that the enemy will often try to besiege us with the greatest attack he can muster right before our breakthrough. The devil cannot read our minds or the mind of God, but he sees in the spirit realm. That's his native habitat, remember? He was kicked out of heaven for wanting to usurp God (Luke 10:18 is a great reference to Jesus having witnessed Satan falling from heaven).

So the devil can detect when the heavenly activity around you is abuzz in preparation for your next awesome Kingdom-Come assignment, and he will do anything he can to stop you. If you are under heavy fire right now, I just want to encourage you and congratulate you. Get ready because your breakthrough is breaking through!

FACE THE ENEMY

ACTIVITY N: Crushing Fear

What are some of your favorite fear-crushing verses? Flip through this book again and list scriptures that you've highlighted and noted through this journey. Make a list of those that have helped you crush fear.

_____

_____

_____

_____

_____

Do a scripture search of your favorite Bible translation for verses on crushing fear and list those as well.

_____

_____

_____

_____

_____

CHAPTER TWENTY-THREE

CRUSH THE ENEMY

"You will trample upon lions and cobras; you will
crush fierce lions and serpents under your feet!"

PSALMS 91:13, NLT

Battle Strategy #3: Slay the Giant

Now that we are better acquainted with our true identity and have taken our stand, even if on wobbly spiritual legs, it's time to slay the giant standing in our way and take possession of the inheritance promised and paid for us.

"But how?" you may be asking.

The Bible says it's the same spirit that raised Christ from the dead that quickens, or makes alive, our mortal bodies (Romans 8:11). It is by grace established in the new covenant of Jesus's blood, the finished work on the cross, that we have the authority and power to overcome all the works of the evil one. Jesus gave us the authority by restoring us as sons and daughters of God. The Holy Spirit produces the power and the results.

> 'Not by might nor by power, but by my Spirit,' says the Lord Almighty. This mountain shall be removed by My spirit, says the Lord of Hosts. What are you mighty mountain? Before Zerubbabel you will become level ground. (Zachariah 4:6-7)

> And I [Jesus] will ask the Father, and he will give you another advocate to help you and be with you forever—the Spirit of truth . . . The Advocate, the Holy Spirit, whom the Father will send in my name,

will teach you all things and will remind you of
everything I have said to you. (John 14:16-17, 26)

No matter how big a mountain the evil one's schemes may seem,
the Holy Spirit enforces its removal by backing up our warfare with
action. The Holy Spirit was sent to teach us in all things, including
how we slay giants and walk into victory. So you see, we cannot lose!

But just standing firm and facing our enemy isn't enough. Now
is the time for offensive attack. In a war, you have to plan your battle
in such a way as to achieve the intended victory, often in a series of
individual attacks that move you forward to your ultimate goal. I'm
going to share here three steps of offensive attack that have helped
me slay my own giants. Again, you may come up with more of your
own. But these will help you get started.

First Attack: Lift Jesus Up

The first offensive attack is to lift Jesus up high over the trauma or
life situation that has caused pain and resulted in fear creeping in. If
you aren't able to trace your fear back to a particular situation, then
lift Jesus up over your family and life history as well as your mind.
The battle for peace is the battle over your mind. Bottom line, the
enemy wants to dominate the thoughts in your mind.

So what does it mean to lift Jesus up? First, the image is of
Jesus being lifted high on the cross so that people can look to him
for salvation, just as Moses was commanded by God to make a
bronze image of a serpent in the wilderness when the disobedient,
complaining Israelites were bitten by serpents, so that any who
had faith to look up at the image would be healed (Numbers 21:9).

And as Moses lifted up the serpent in the wilderness,
even so must the Son of man be lifted up. (John 3:14)

> And when I [Jesus] am lifted up from the earth, I
> will draw everyone to myself. (John 12:32)

Jesus is the atonement for all our sins, consequences of sin, and record of debt produced by all sin committed past, present, and future. He fulfilled all requirements of the law of sin and death by becoming our sin and overcoming death, hell, and the grave. But the image of lifting Jesus up is not just of Jesus on the cross. Isaiah 6:1 describes "the Lord, high and exalted, seated on a throne; and the train of his robe filled the temple."

This is significant to me because the Bible tells us that we as God's children are his temple (1 Corinthians 3:16-17; 6:19-20). The train of his robe symbolizes his presence filling his temple—us! Isaiah goes on to describe Jesus as a banner lifted high for all the nations to see.

> On that day the root of Jesse [Jesus] will **stand as a
> banner** for the peoples. The nations will seek him,
> and his place of rest will be glorious. (Isaiah 11:10)

The image here is of the special flag that is lifted above the king in battle or above his castle when he is in residence to let all who see it know that the king is present. When Jesus is lifted high, the nations will seek him. And wherever he is present will be a glorious place of rest for his people. The apostle Paul in his epistle to the Philippians also describes Jesus lifted high so that all people will bow and worship.

> **God exalted him to the highest place** and gave
> him the name that is above every name, that at the
> name of Jesus every knee should bow, in heaven
> and on earth and under the earth, and every tongue
> acknowledge that Jesus Christ is Lord, to the glory
> of God the Father. (Philippians 2:9-11)

CRUSH THE ENEMY

When we lift Jesus up as king of all, even over our current situations and circumstances, we are placing him where he rightfully belongs—as our Savior, Redeemer, and Healer. What is exciting about this is that when we place Jesus where he belongs on **his** throne, he enables us as his co-heirs to do the incredible things he did while living on this earth. In fact, he promises that as his followers we have the power to do even greater things than we see Jesus doing in the gospels.

> Very truly I tell you, whoever believes in me will do the works I have been doing, and they will do even greater things than these, because I am going to the Father. And I will do whatever you ask in my name, so that the Father may be glorified in the Son. You may ask me for anything in my name, and I will do it. (John 14:12-14)

Did you catch that? You, yes YOU, are to do even greater things than Jesus did because your Redeemer is in heaven backing you up! So rebuke that spirit of oppression and fear in Jesus's name. Say it out loud and with authority: "Devil, I see what you are doing, and I bind you, spirit of oppression and fear, and all your demons in Jesus's name. I rebuke you in Jesus's name and cast you into dry uninhabitable places. Go now!!"

Now maybe you have a hard time believing you could possibly do what Jesus did, much less even greater things. I just want to encourage you right now that if you're feeling instability or insecurity in your faith, you are in good company. My faith has certainly been shaky many times at best. But Jesus himself promised that we only need a tiny bit of faith no bigger than a mustard seed to move entire mountains in his name.

> And Jesus rebuked the demon, and it came out of him, and the boy was healed instantly. Then the disciples came to Jesus privately and said, "Why

could we not cast it out?" He said to them, "Because of your little faith. For truly, I say to you, **if you have faith like a grain of mustard seed, you will say to this mountain, 'Move from here to there,' and it will move,** and nothing will be impossible for you." (Matthew 17:18-20)

Have you ever seen a mustard seed? They are miniscule! And notice the rest of Jesus's promise. It's not just mountains we can move. Nothing is impossible when we keep our eyes fixed on our lifted-up King and ask in his name.

But notice too that the promise Jesus made of his followers doing even greater things than he did while on earth was in context to doing the works the Father called him to do and glorifying the Father. His promise isn't some kind of genie-in-a-bottle wish for whatever you want and you'll get it. That would be pretty selfish and quickly abused. What Jesus is promising is that when his followers are out there doing the Father's works to bring glory to the Father, we have only to ask with as much faith as a mustard seed, and he will bestow his *dunamis* power through God's Holy Spirit to do great and mighty things, including miracles, for the furtherance of God's kingdom on earth (Mark 16:17-18).

Second Attack: Eat to Build Strength

Psalm 23, often called the Shepherd's Psalm, was written by King David with imagery of his own youth as a shepherd. It describes God as the Good Shepherd and us as the sheep. Verse 5 states: "You prepare a table before me in the presence of my enemies."

I used to wonder why God would be preparing a meal for his flock in the middle of enemy territory. Then it hit me that this means our enemy, the devil, must watch us sit down, relax, and eat with complete safety in the care of our Good Shepherd.

What are we eating at this table under God's protection in the presence of our enemies? We're eating God's Word. Just as a sword is used as a symbol of God's Word being utilized as an offensive weapon, so the imagery of food is used for our partaking of God's Word.

> Like newborn babies, **long for the pure milk of the word,** so that by it you may grow in respect to salvation. (1 Peter 2:2)

> Then I will give you shepherds after My own heart, **who will feed you on knowledge and understanding.** (Jeremiah 3:15)

> I [Jesus] **am the living bread** that came down out of heaven; **if anyone eats of this bread,** he will live forever. (John 6:51)

> **Your words were found and I ate them,** and Your word became to me the gladness and joy of my heart. (Jeremiah 15:16)

> For though by this time you ought to be teachers, you have need again for someone to teach you the elementary principles of the oracles of God, and you have come to **need milk and not solid food.** For everyone who partakes only of milk is not accustomed to the word of righteousness, for he is an infant. But **solid food is for the mature,** who because of practice have their senses trained to discern good and evil. (Hebrews 5:12-14)

So what is our second stage of attack? Eat! Eat the Word of God day and night. Just graze and feed on it. Every chance you get, get the Word in you. If you are super-busy like most of us, subscribe to devotionals and get updates on your phone. I get Joseph Prince's daily devotionals. They are awesome! Surround yourself with the

Word. Here's the key. It's not so much about you getting into the Word as it is the Word getting into you!

I remember the first several weeks after we moved to Florida. The panic attacks were numerous. I could hardly look out the windows of our temporary apartment without being overwhelmed by all the unknowns of our circumstances. When I tried to leave the apartment, I was frequently overwhelmed by all the errands and tasks I had to complete to meet the basic needs for my little children, and I'd have another panic attack. Any time I passed by a mirror, I could see a face of pain, rejection, and fear that belonged to me.

So I wouldn't have to look at that face, I desperately wrote scriptures all over the windows and mirrors in the apartment. The Word that had been instilled into my spirit began to bubble out without me even opening the Bible. Here are just a few of the verses I posted. From prior chapters, you will know why these in particular were significant to me.

> The chastisement for my peace was upon Jesus, and by his stripes I am healed. (Isaiah 53:5)

> God hasn't given me a spirit of fear and timidity, but that of love and of power and a strong balanced mind. (2 Timothy 1:7)

> My peace I leave with you, my peace I give to you, it's not the peace this world knows. (John 14:27)

> No weapon formed against me will prosper. Every tongue that rises up against me, you will condemn. (Isaiah 54:17)

> You are my hiding place. You protect me from trouble; you surround me with songs of deliverance. (Psalms 32:7)

The scriptures I scribbled were life to me. I needed the Word of God as much as I needed oxygen in my lungs. I didn't always copy them out perfectly or even have the Bible reference associated with each scripture. At that time, I was so sick at heart that eating was difficult. So I made it a practice to "eat" the scriptures I'd written on the windows and mirrors. I'd whisper them, repeating them over and over. When terror struck, and it did continually, I'd have the promises of God on my lips.

As we consume the Word and bask in the presence of Jesus, the Holy Spirit in us fans the flames of the living Word of God, activating them and making them come into fruition in us and around us. And this is all because of the goodness and grace from our Father God. Remember that the Word is alive and active!

> For the word of God is living and active, sharper
> than any two-edged sword, piercing to the division
> of soul and of spirit, of joints and of marrow, and
> discerning the thoughts and intentions of the heart.
> (Hebrews 4:12)

The Word of God is strategically removing the pain and trauma in our souls and revealing our true godly nature in our spirit man. The Word is superfood for our spirits and souls. It builds spiritual muscle, empowers us to walk in supernatural peace and power, and strengthens us for long distances.

Third Attack: Speak the Word Out

The words we speak are a mighty offensive attack against the devil's works. Remember, the power of life or death are in the tongue (Proverbs 18:21). We spoke earlier about Jesus facing Satan's temptations in the wilderness. Each time Satan offered a temptation, Jesus responded by pointing the devil back to the Word of God.

It is written, man shall not live on bread alone, but
on every word that comes from the mouth of God.
(Matthew 4:4)

The enemy loves to use a fearful opportunity to unleash more
and more fear scenarios until you are hamstrung, crippled in fear.
The wonderful truth is that over ninety percent of these fear scenarios
will never ever come true. The devil is the biggest liar. And he attacks
with fear to keep you stuck, to keep you from having hope, and to
keep you from crushing his tactics.

But God's Spirit-breathed Word gives us all the ammunition we
need to slay fear. When you proclaim and decree the Word of God,
you crush the enemy's tactics. Instead of you being crippled in fear,
you crush fear. You yank fear right out of your mind and heart and
place it back under the feet of Jesus, right back where it belongs.

As you begin consuming the Word, release the power of the
Word by implementing the most powerful weapon in your arsenal—
your tongue. Did you know the tongue is actually described as a
dangerous weapon? It can be used for blessing or for cursing and
destruction (James 3:5-9). I already shared the impact on our family
when I used my tongue to give voice to my fears over our failure-to-
thrive son's health.

Used positively, speaking God's Word out loud is a powerful
weapon. Remember that it is our offensive weapon, the sword of
the Spirit (Ephesians 6:17), alive and active, able to penetrate our
thoughts and attitudes of the heart (Hebrews 4:12-13).

So go on the attack with God's Word. Read the Word out loud.
Quote the Word out loud. Even very quietly is powerful and effective.
Speak the Word of God over yourself continually. The Bible says to
meditate on the Word. The literal Hebrew meaning of "meditate' is
to mutter audibly. Even when you can't read it or speak it, keep the
Word of God flowing into you. At night, put your earbuds in and
find some fear-conquering scriptures to speak over you as you sleep.
Your spirit, now united with the Holy Spirit within you, does not

sleep. Feed your spirit the everlasting Word of God day and night, night and day even as you sleep.

Keep God's Promises on Your Lips

For another example of victory in seemingly impossible battles, we can look at Joshua, who had inherited from Moses the responsibility of leading the Israelites into the Promised Land, a beautiful land but one where they would be facing powerful enemies and even giants (Numbers 13:33). God gave Joshua the following mandate.

> Be strong and courageous, because you will lead these people to inherit the land I swore to their ancestors to give them. Be strong and very courageous. Be careful to obey all the law my servant Moses gave you; do not turn from it to the right or to the left, that you may be successful wherever you go. **Keep this Book of the Law always on your lips; meditate on it day and night** so that you may be careful to do everything written in it. Then you will be prosperous and successful. Have I not commanded you? Be strong and courageous. **Do not be afraid;** do not be discouraged, for the Lord your God will be with you wherever you go. (Joshua 1:6-9)

This event took place about two thousand years before Jesus fulfilled the law spoken of in these passages. But notice that then like now God's instructions are to keep the Word always on our mind and on our lips. God was basically telling Joshua and the Israelite people to not allow the enemy to discount their identity, purpose, and inheritance as God's chosen people through his favorite tactic of fear. Our God is the same yesterday, today, and forever! Amen?

Let's recap. What was the Israelites' identity? Children of God.

What was their inheritance? God's promises. What was their purpose? Possess the Promised Land.

What is our identity today? Sons and daughters of God. What is our inheritance? God's promises as co-heirs with Jesus. What is our purpose? With courage and faith and the authority we have as children of God, we too can possess the land of peace and prosperity promised to us. We take possession even though the land is filled with giants as it was for Joshua. We take it one forward step at a time. Those giants aren't so formidable when we know who's holding the promissory note—our Father God!

Do not allow the enemy to discredit your identity. Jesus paid a horrific price for it. Do not allow the enemy to discount your destiny, purpose, or calling. To do so discounts the blood of Jesus. On the cross our Savior conquered the enemy and all the enemy's works and tactics, including fear. Speak out his promises! Make declarations! Walk forward! Possess the land!

ACTIVITY O: Facing Down Our Giants

Have you ever felt like David or Joshua facing a giant many times your size and strength? If so, think about the following questions and answer them as fully as possible. Use your journal if you need more space.

Who or what is the Goliath in your life today?

_____

_____

David had faith God would help him defeat Goliath because he'd witnessed God's faithfulness and power in helping him defeat much smaller bears and lions. Are there some bears and lions God has already aided you in taking down? If so, describe them here.

_____

_____

Do you think God will help you take down the Goliath? Why or why not?

_____

_____

_____

CHAPTER TWENTY-FOUR

ABIDE

"He who dwells in the secret place of the Most High shall abide under the shadow of the Almighty. I will say of the Lord, 'He is my refuge and my fortress; My God, in Him I will trust.'"

PSALMS 91:1-2, NKJV

Battle Strategy #4: Abide in the Secret Place and Enter into Rest

We've faced down the giant and defeated our enemy with the Word of God. Our foe is defeated and under Jesus's feet. Now we enter into the "secret place of the Most High" (Psalm 91:1, NKJV). Does it seem counterproductive to be ducking down into some secret place instead of waging war against people and circumstances, fighting for your rights, telling it like it is, demanding answers, respect, and apologies? Do you feel victimized if you don't stand up and fight? What kind of strategy is this?

Let me assure you that entering into rest and remaining at rest is not passivity. So let's just pivot the battlefield on its axis a bit and reassess. What if we take a step back and let the Great Defender and Deliverer fight for us? Is that not an effective strategy? After all, is our Father God not the greatest of all Avengers?

In truth, rest can be very active. While defeated, the enemy is still trying to launch projectiles of doubt, temptations to fear, distracting memories, and whispers of accusations. Hebrews 4:11 says about the Sabbath-rest of God's people entering the Promised Land, "Let us, therefore, **make every effort** to enter that rest." The King James Version words it, "Let us **labor** therefore to enter into that rest."

Laboring and making every effort are extremely active verbs.

In fact, they describe someone working really hard. Who would have thought that it takes hard work to enter into rest, to abide in God's secret place? But rest is a proactive choice. It means resisting temptation to enter back into oppression and fear. It means deliberately placing that oppression and fear right back on Jesus.

Rest is where intimacy increases. Where trust, which equals faith, grows. This is the place where we receive love and identity and value from our Savior and Father. We must receive from Jesus in a place of rest in order to have faith, strength, insight, and strategy for the fiery darts that lay ahead. And all we really have to do is surrender our own constant struggle of why and how.

Just visualize that familiar biblical image of Jesus as the Good Shepherd carrying a little fluffy white lamb on his broad, strong shoulders (Luke 15:3-7). That little lamb did have to do something in order to be carried. The little lamb had to come into agreement with the shepherd. The lamb had to consent to be still and be carried through the rough terrain back to the flock, back to safety.

It's the same with you and me. When we find that we're struggling with the circumstances of our reality, STOP! Be still! Place your struggle, the fears, the whys, and the hows all at the feet of Jesus. Let Jesus pick you up and carry you through the rough patch even if the rough patch stretches out as far as your eyes can see. Your Papa God has a plan, and it is so much better than you could ever imagine!

When an attack comes—and I say when, not if, because they will come—we can see the enemy's strategy for what it is—whether distraction, disappointment, hurt, rejection, failure. If our emotions try to tell us we're stuck with this attack, that we have to carry our fears instead of letting Jesus carry us, then we must change our stinkin' thinkin'!

That's essentially what it means to repent. The full Greek meaning for the word repent (remember that the New Testament was originally written in Greek) means "to change your mind." What does that look like? We dispute and rebuke those thoughts that aren't from God by capturing and casting down any thoughts that exalt themselves over what God's plan is for our lives, what Jesus paid for, and what the living Word of God says about us. The apostle Paul sums it up like this:

> For though we live in the world, we do not wage war as the world does. The weapons we fight with are not the weapons of the world. On the contrary, they have divine power to demolish strongholds. We demolish arguments and every pretension that sets itself up against the knowledge of God, and we take captive every thought to make it obedient to Christ. (2 Corinthians 10:3-5)

In our previous battle strategy, we stepped forward in battle. We took back the peace that the enemy had stolen. We repossessed our rightful identity. We likely still don't have all the answers to the endless questions running through our minds. Here's the deal. We aren't going to get all the answers to our many why and how questions. We just aren't.

But Papa God has such a way of fading those questions all to black the way a movie screen fades to a distant backdrop in order to then illuminate the glorious unfolding of our—YOUR—very real and near future. All the promises yet to come. All the wonders of his love coming to fruition in you. All the redemption, favor, success, and joy about to explode in your innermost sanctum. Let's take a closer look at Psalms 91 in the context of finding our rest and refuge in our heavenly Father. This time I am using *The Passion Translation*, a newer, heart-level paraphrase by biblical scholar Brian Simmons.

Psalm 91: Safe and Secure

> When you sit enthroned under the shadow of Shaddai, you are hidden in the strength of God Most High. He's the hope that holds me and the Stronghold to shelter me, the only God for me, and

my great confidence. He will rescue you from every
hidden trap of the enemy, and he will protect you
from false accusation and any deadly curse. (vv.1-3)

What does this mean? What does it look like to sit in the shadow
of God? To better understand that, let's take a look at one of the
names for God referenced in this verse: Shaddai. Other versions use
the name El Shaddai. "El" translates to "God" or "Lord." Shaddai is
commonly translated as "Almighty." Further investigation reveals
that the root word for Shaddai is "Shadad," which translates as
"destroyer." So El Shaddai is Almighty God the Destroyer! Now it
makes sense when we read further in the verse, "you are hidden in
the strength of God Most High."

Picture this. When we are covered by the shadow of something,
this generally means that the something covering us is much larger
than we are and very, very near. When we are tucked in under the
shadow like children under a comforting blanket or chicks under
their mother's wings, we are enthroned in a place of holiness, nestled
down under the protection of our Almighty Destroyer of giants.
What a Father!

By the way, did you read in these verses that Almighty Destroyer
would deliver you from *some* of the traps of the enemy? A *few* false
accusations? Maybe *one or two* deadly curses? Read it again. The text
says every single one!

His massive arms are wrapped around you,
protecting you. You can run under his covering of
majesty and hide. His arms of faithfulness are a
shield keeping you from harm. You will never worry
about an attack of demonic forces at night nor have
to fear a spirit of darkness coming against you. Don't
fear a thing! Whether by night or by day, demonic
danger will not trouble you, nor will the powers of
evil launched against you. (vv. 4-6)

I was just reminded of the importance of this passage today. It has been a busy season in our family as we've just stepped into a new ministry—foster parenting. A four-month-old precious baby girl came to us on a Wednesday night already sick. By Friday she was very sick. I stayed with her one night in the hospital, then Scott stayed with her a second night.

It didn't help when our son brought a virus home from a visit to see our new family member in the hospital. During this bout with illness, he had two small seizures. We'd thought he'd been delivered from seizures once and for all. Fear, frustration, despair, and defeat tried to steal the day. The devil throws fiery darts, especially when we are stepping out into ministry and when we are exhausted.

Exhausted is exactly what I was feeling when on top of everything else the enemy planted a bad dream that tempted me to tailspin into my historic ways of stinkin' thinkin'. It was a distinct reminder of the horrible pain that in the past had always erupted into panic attacks. I got up the next morning a little frustrated but was reminded that just as we tuck into bed each night, I needed to tuck into the secret place of the Almighty Destroyer, Abba Father.

Isn't this GREAT news? We can take off our boxing gloves, hop into our jammies, and go to sleep at night knowing that our Almighty Destroyer Father is watching over us. We can count on him to keep our defenses and crush the enemy's power. The enemy will try to tempt us, but he has no power over us. Almighty, All-Powerful Abba himself towers over us and keeps us safe.

> Even in a time of disaster, with thousands and thousands being killed, you will remain unscathed and unharmed. You will be a spectator as the wicked perish in judgment, for they will be paid back for what they have done! (vv. 7-8)

To further liberate us from captivity and bondage, we are going to forgive and set free those who have hurt us. We will discuss this in detail later on. In our forgiveness we are going to free the person or people from the punishment of their injustices and injury. So it is not they whom we wish to see destroyed, rather the enemy who is the cause for injury.

> When we live our lives within the shadow of God Most High, our secret hiding place, we will always be shielded from harm. How then could evil prevail against us or disease infect us? God sends angels with special orders to protect you wherever you go, defending you from all harm. If you walk into a trap, they'll be there for you and keep you from stumbling. You'll even walk unharmed among the fiercest powers of darkness, trampling every one of them beneath your feet! For here is what the Lord has spoken to me: "Because you have delighted in me as my great lover, I will greatly protect you. I will set you in a high place, safe and secure before my face. [Other translations say, "I will set you on high and honor you."] I will answer your cry for help every time you pray, and you will find and feel my presence even in your time of pressure and trouble. I will be your glorious hero and give you a feast. You will be satisfied with a full life and with all that I do for you. For you will enjoy the fullness of my salvation! (vv. 9-16)

Oh how glorious! This chapter has been a complete game-changer for me in my darkest hours when all hope was lost. This chapter breathed life and love into my helpless situation. I didn't necessarily expect that my immediate situation was going to radically change so much. I just wasn't there yet. But I did experience peace and love. And that gave me hope and a trust that I was not alone. That Abba, Daddy God himself, had run to my rescue and was raising me up high over the situation just as he promised. That all would be well because I was safe in his arms.

What is our Father God asking us to do? Sit down in a place of protection, rest, and righteousness in his covering. Be still and do not fear. You know your true identity. Meditate on it daily. In fact, several times a day.

Now this is beginning to sound a bit prescriptive. So I must emphasize the key. The one thing we seek after forever more is intimacy. It is in his presence, in the secret place, that the Lord God himself gives you discernment, teaches you about his plans, and gives you visions. It is where he downloads gifts like ingenious strategies, creative inventions, greater awareness of himself, greater peace, greater faith, and more strengths and talents than we ever imagined. The Word of God promises that we can experience God's presence without measure. Let's go after his presence with all our might. In his secret place nothing else can touch us except more of him, more of his presence, and more of his glory!

CHAPTER TWENTY-FIVE

HOLY SPIRIT

"But I tell you the truth, it is to your advantage that I go away; for if I do not go away, the Helper (Comforter, Advocate, Intercessor—Counselor, Strengthener, Standby) will not come to you; but if I go, I will send Him (the Holy Spirit) to you [to be in close fellowship with you]."

JOHN 16:7, AMP

Battle Strategy #5: Partner and Participate with the Holy Spirit

In the first chapter of Acts, Jesus had risen from the dead. Over a forty-day period, he appeared to his disciples along with more than five hundred other believers (1 Corinthians 15:6). He taught them about his kingdom and instructed the disciples that they were to go throughout the world to share the good news of his resurrection. But first, they were to remain in Jerusalem until they received the gift Jesus had promised before his death of a Helper, Advocate, Teacher, and Comforter (John 14:16, 26; 15:26; 16:7-15).

> Do not leave Jerusalem, but wait for the gift my Father promised, which you have heard me speak about. For John baptized with water, but in a few days you will be baptized with the Holy Spirit. (Acts 1:4-5)

Why did the disciples and other believers need to be filled with the power of the Holy Spirit? Because they were going to face opposition and heavy persecution. They needed the power, wisdom, and discernment of the Holy Spirit to complete their mission. It is the same with you and me.

Understand this, dear reader. We are in a fight. A fight to the finish-line of this life. We must be indwelt and filled to overflowing with the Holy Spirit to triumph well. The enemy will come back again and again, using the bait of fear, distraction, discouragement, disappointment, accusation, and other identity-shaking deceit to see if he can get us back on his hook. But all that we need to succeed and win this fight is already within us. When we understand our identity and inheritance through Jesus Christ, then by his grace we will not take the bait. And if we do, the Holy Spirit will help us discern the truth so we can get right back off that hook.

> But the Advocate, the **Holy Spirit**, whom the Father will send in my name, **will teach you all things** and will remind you of everything I have said to you. (John 14:26)

So what is our fifth battle strategy? To partner and participate with the Spirit of God. Every morning before your feet even hit the floor, make a point to greet the Holy Spirit and invite him to participate with each moment of your day. Ask him to teach you all things you need to be aware of for the day. To help you make decisions and process information. To increase his presence in your life. To develop your character so that it produces Holy Spirit fruit. The apostle Paul's epistle to the Galatians gives us a list of that fruit.

> But the fruit of the Spirit is **love, joy, peace, forbearance, kindness, goodness, faithfulness** and **self-control**. Against such things there is no law. (Galatians 5:22-23)

You are cultivating a relationship with the Holy Spirit, so don't forget to speak to him throughout the day. It is the Holy Spirit living within us who gives us blessed assurance, peace, joy, and above all, power to overcome all obstacles in life.

And if **the Spirit of him who raised Jesus from the dead is living in you**, he who raised Christ from the dead will also give life to your mortal bodies because of **his Spirit who lives in you**. For those who are led by **the Spirit of God** are the children of God. (Romans 8:13-14)

Don't you know that you yourselves are God's temple and that **God's Spirit dwells in your midst**? (1 Corinthians 3:16)

If the Holy Spirit is living in us, that means we are inseparable. You might call us BFFs (Best Friends Forever). As our BFF, the Holy Spirit wants to be incorporated into every detail of our daily lives, no matter how insignificant we may think it. In fact, we should be so observant and yielded to the Holy Spirit's input and influence that our fleshly self (that's the emotions, thinking, reasoning part of us) takes a back seat. Holy Spirit, PLEASE take the wheel!

Value and Prioritize the Holy Spirit's Presence

How do we cultivate a relationship with the Spirit of God? Just spend time soaking in his presence. Listen to what he is speaking to you in his soft, still voice. Get to know him through his Word.

I'm not denying we all have a ton on our plates. We absolutely do! What I'm saying is that we need to prioritize our quiet time, our abiding in that "secret place." That doesn't mean we don't get up and go to work. But we need to set aside our quiet time with God before the day begins. Think of it as your first garment, your first article of spiritual armor you are going to dress in for the day. If we don't do this first thing, that early morning meeting, errand running, endless inbox and electronic distractions can gobble us up and sabotage our time before we can even think about it.

Another way I love to experience the Spirit of God is through worship. The Bible says that God inhabits the praise of his people (Psalms 22:3, KJV). Since the Holy Spirit is the member of the Trinity who indwells us, that's talking about him! As you worship, you'll find that you feel his presence in such tangible ways you may never want to leave that place. Of course you have to eventually leave physically. But you can take that place with you in your heart everywhere you go throughout the day. When you find yourself missing that Holy Spirit presence, retrain the focus of your heart and get right back inside your "secret place" again.

By increasing intimacy with the Holy Spirit, we also increase his jurisdiction and power within us. As his presence in us increases, the darkness around us decreases. Where there is light, darkness is expelled. This is how you and I shut down evil forces. How we disarm the enemy with our very presence. The quantity and quality of the Spirit of God in us is greater and mightier than the darkness around us (1 John 4:4-6, 13). There is coming a generation of powerful sons and daughters of God who dispel darkness and usher in peace because they have allowed the Holy Spirit to be poured out within them (Joel 2:28-29, Acts 2:16-18). I am claiming that for you and for me! Amen?

ACTIVITY P: Staying in Jerusalem

The disciples were eager and ready after forty days of final instruction from the risen Jesus to begin their mission, their Great Commission, of taking the Good News to the nations. But Jesus commanded them to wait patiently in Jerusalem until they received the anointing of the Holy Spirit that would empower them to reach the nations. We too need that anointing as well as to discern God's timing and direction. Ponder what God's call is for your own life as you answer the following questions. If you need more room, use your journal.

What is your Jerusalem? Where is the Lord asking you to remain, stay the course, be steadfast when you'd much rather run away, hair on fire?

_____

_____

_____

If the Lord is with you, are you willing to remain in your Jerusalem until you are filled with power from the Holy Spirit?

_____

_____

_____

CHAPTER TWENTY-SIX

PEACE

"May the God of hope fill you with all joy and peace
as you trust in him, so that you may overflow
with hope by the power of the Holy Spirit."

ROMANS 15:13

Battle Strategy #6: Safeguard Your Peace

When I think of safeguarding my peace, I think of a soldier walking around the boundary of a military fortress. Within that boundary is a safe place where I live with my family. There we worship, love, laugh, and are at peace.

It isn't enough to just conduct self-checks on your peace levels as we discussed in chapter twenty-one. We must actively seek to preserve, protect, and defend our peace. I can't stress too strongly this part of the battle plan because we just don't do it nearly enough. In a modern society full of electronics, agendas, and efficiencies, we cram more into our daily schedule than is intelligent. Being a "go get 'er" kind of girl, I used to be the absolute worst at this and still have to vigilantly monitor it to this day. I love rolling up my sleeves and jumping into any task. But this often results in "work harder, not smarter" outcomes with plenty of mistakes and smudgy-gray lines of peace and rest.

The truth is that for every commitment we say yes to, something else in our lives gets a no. Think of it like an economics class. You have a yes account and a no account. At the end of a time period, these two accounts must be reconciled. Ideally, you want your no account to be on the plus side of the ledger. Your no account is your balance of peace, which is a gift from God, as we see in the following verses.

Let the **peace of Christ** rule in your hearts, since
as members of one body you were called to peace.
(Colossians 3:15)

The **peace of God**, which transcends all understanding, will guard your hearts and your minds in
Christ Jesus. (Philippians 4:7)

You [God] will keep in **perfect peace** those whose
minds are steadfast, because they trust in you.
(Isaiah 26:3)

Now may **the Lord of peace himself give you peace**
at all times and in every way. (2 Thessalonians 3:16)

Notice that our peace is God's peace and bestowed on us by God.
But we are told to let that peace rule. To guard our hearts, which
Christ has filled with his peace. To have steadfast minds in order to
keep that perfect peace. All of which requires action and decisions
on our part to safeguard that peace and not let it be frittered away.

It may at first seem selfish to be striving for a no balance instead
of a yes balance. But it is from this reservoir of peace that we are able
to be an effective instrument of God's glory, bringing his kingdom
to this earth. This in turn benefits your family members, friends,
associates, and all those in your sphere of influence. Which brings
me to my next point.

Value YOU!

Yeah, I said that! Don't exhaust your valuable resources—time,
peace, energy, and resources—on people who misuse or manipulate
you or your time. There will be situations when dealing with
family members, colleagues, and close friends where you'll have to
navigate with caution. Ask the Holy Spirit to give you wisdom in

handling these situations. But don't be a dumping ground for gossip or haphazard emotional waste. That is simply not your spiritual jurisdiction. Repeat after me (I'm pretty sure I borrowed this from Havilah Cunnington, who is an amazing minister of the Word): "My ears are not your dumpsters!"

Of course, you must use wisdom and discernment here. When you get caught up in drama, ask questions such as the following:

- Lord, how do you want to use me in this situation?
- Other than praying, am I able to make a difference?
- Is this an opportunity to showcase Jesus?
- Is this person (or people) able or willing to receive what you have to say through me?

If the answer is no, ask the person or people if you can pray with them. If they agree, pray right there on the spot for peace and for God's presence to penetrate the situation. Then move the discussion along to something else.

When I find myself in such a situation, I typically will wait for a natural break in the action such as the person taking a breath or a thinking pause. If it becomes clear the person isn't going to pause, I will jump in with some words of empathy like: "Oh my goodness, I'm so sorry. That's just terrible. I can only imagine what you must be going through. This sounds like a job only God Almighty can do, but he is in the miracle-working business! Can I pray with you?"

If I have a *brief* testimony that is applicable, I will share it, then with some kind parting words, move away from that person/ situation.

Value Your Imagination

It is also vital to safeguard your imagination. I don't open up my imagination to anything that doesn't bring peace. Whether videos or books, whether romance, drama, suspense, action, or thrillers, I will not allow anything on my spiritual menu that might leave dribbles, smudges, and smears of garbage on my imagination. I'm pretty militant on this, but desperate times call for desperate measures! I'm not saying you have to do what I do. But I am suggesting that if you find your imagination replaying scenarios from action/sex/drama/horror scenes that counteract peace, you might want to reconsider how you are investing your time or populating your imagination.

Your imagination is a powerful tool. It is the "silver screen" of your purpose and destiny. Whatever we feed our imaginations grows into our reality. God gave us our imagination for a wonderful purpose—to dream dreams of purpose and calling with him. It is through our imagination that God develops his kingdom-come perspective, scenes, script, and plot in each of us. My "silver screen" is where I go for the Holy Spirit to communicate with me. Where I dream of tucking into the very heartbeat of Father God to see what's on his heart, feel what he feels, and do what he wants me to do about it. This is the place I go to dance with Jesus and worship him.

Washing of the Word

But what about the crud that has already gotten into our minds? How do we get that back out so as to restore our peace? The Bible tells us how to do that as well. We just have to go back to the section on slaying our giants and the offensive weapon God gave us to do that—his Word. God's Word isn't just a sword to fight the enemy and food to nourish our soul. It is also the world's best detergent as the apostle Paul describes.

> Husbands, love your wives, just as Christ loved the church and gave himself up for her to make her holy, cleansing her by the **washing with water through the Word**. (Ephesians 5:25-26)

We aren't just surrounded by gossip and emotional drama that can steal our peace. We also live in a modern world that is spilling over maximum capacity with news, information, and sensationalism, much of which also is also peace-stealing. So it is paramount that we take time to clean our minds through the washing of the Word. The more we fill our minds with God's Word, the less room peace-stealing thoughts and images will have to take up residency there. Listen to what *The Passion Translation* has to say about the effect of God's Word has on our hearts, minds, and souls and why safeguarding our inner refuge of peace is so important.

> Listen carefully, my dear child, to everything that I teach you, and pay attention to all that I have to say. **Fill your thoughts with my words** until they penetrate deep into your spirit. Then, as you unwrap my words, **they will impart true life and radiant health into the very core of your being.** So above all, guard the affections of your heart, for **they affect all that you are. Pay attention to the welfare of your innermost being, for from there flows the wellspring of life.** (Proverbs 4:20-23)

Wise Counsel

I would also like to emphasize how critical it is to listen to the right kind of counsel. May I recommend you deliberately seek out at least one person to be a consistent source of wise counsel in your life. For me that has been my sister Ashley. During the most difficult season of my life, she was there every day by phone, helping me work through the major obstacles and routine small hurdles. She was and still is my wisest counsel and best ally. She helps me remain focused on the bigger picture, the bigger prize of overcoming, of bringing the kingdom of heaven to our home—and to life at large.

The person you choose as your wise counsel should be someone who knows and loves Jesus with all their heart. This person is not typically our best friend, work associate, or other social acquaintance. It should be a person with no ulterior motive other than to see you succeed, overcome, and carry forward the commission Jesus has called, empowered, and anointed you to complete. Our heavenly Father will ensure the right person is put in your path. Perhaps you already have a spiritual mom, dad, brother, or sister in your life. If you don't, ask your church leadership if there is such a person they can recommend. Many churches even have spiritual mentoring ministries that will assign an older-in-the-faith, more spiritually mature Christian, preferably of your own gender (Titus 2:3-5, 2 Timothy 2:2), to be that ongoing wise counsel in your life.

Battle Strategy #7: Fix Your Eyes on Jesus Your High Priest

Battle strategy #7, which is our final battle strategy, in effect makes possible all the others. Whether standing our ground, fighting our giants, laboring to enter our place of rest, immersing ourselves in God's Word, prayer, and/or worship, we need to keep our focus where it needs to be—on our wonderful Savior, great High Priest, Healer, Advocate before the Father, and co-heir Jesus Christ. We've already talked a lot about what Jesus has done for us, what our inheritance is in him, and much more. But let's take a look quickly at two passages that make clear why keeping our focus on Jesus is so important to our victory.

> Let us throw off everything that hinders and the sin that so easily entangles. And let us run with perseverance the race marked out for us, **fixing our eyes on Jesus**, the pioneer and perfecter of faith. For the joy set before him he endured the cross, scorning its shame, and sat down at the right hand of the throne of God. Consider him who endured such opposition

from sinners, **so that you will not grow weary and lose heart**. (Hebrews 12:1-3)

Therefore, since we have a great high priest who has ascended into heaven, Jesus the Son of God, let us hold firmly to the faith we profess. For we do not have a high priest who is unable to empathize with our weaknesses, but **we have one [high priest] who has been tempted in every way, just as we are—yet he did not sin**. Let us then approach God's throne of grace with confidence, **so that we may receive mercy and find grace to help us in our time of need**. (Hebrews 4:14-16)

The Bible tells us that we can expect to go through difficult times and face really hard things. Many of us have encountered the valleys of the shadow of death where one moment you're afraid you will surely die and the next moment you're afraid you won't get off that easy. There are times, events, choices, memories in our human frailty that we'd just rather not discuss or disclose because of our sense of failure, fear, shame, and dread.

The good news is that we aren't alone. Jesus has endured opposition, pain, betrayal, shame, and every other hard time we've been through, so he knows exactly how we feel. And because Jesus underwent temptation, though without ever giving into it, he empathizes with our own weaknesses and is there to help us in time of need. But Jesus also overcame all these things, emerging victorious to sit down at the right hand of our heavenly Father.

We can't overcome these things on our own. We can't defeat the enemy on our own. But because Jesus did overcome, because he did defeat the enemy, because he is our great high priest and we are his co-heirs, we can march right up to the throne of God and confidently ask and receive mercy, grace, and help to win our own battle against the enemy.

Isn't that a wonderful assurance to wrap our confidence around!

The devil wants to keep us focused on negative circumstances and feelings of failure, guilt, and shame. If he can accomplish this, he can keep God's truth of grace, peace, and love hidden from our eyes. He can mask God's intended purpose for us and delay our intended destiny.

But the devil is a liar! Remember that grace, hope, and love are a Person. A Person whose name is Jesus. He renews, restores, revives, resuscitates, and resurrects you. His finished work on the cross establishes you as an heir to Father God.

Are you ready to take your place as an heir of God? Then simply fix your eyes on Jesus and run this life's race with perseverance. Why is fixing our eyes on Jesus so important? Because as long as our eyes are focused on our Savior, then they won't be focused on all the pain, grief, failure, and other negativity all around us that can make us grow weary and lose heart.

ACTIVITY Q: Your Battle Plan

We've now walked through the seven strategies of the battle plan my heavenly Father gave to me along with any number of individual battle tactics and practical aids that have helped me not only stand my ground and face my fears but go on the offensive to defeat my enemy in the name of my Savior Jesus Christ and the *dunamis* power of God's Holy Spirit. Now it is time for you to draw up your own battle plan.

First, spend time in prayer asking God's Holy Spirit to reveal to you his specific battle plan for your life. Review all the words from God and insights you've written in the activity sections or your journal. Then with God's help and insight, write out the battle plan God has for you. Feel free to use all or part of mine and anything else you've learned along our journey together. You may end up with a battle plan very similar to mine or with new and different insights. Either way I'd love to learn from you regarding your battleplan and journey, so feel free to drop me an email at ***prayer@ greaterthingstoday.com*** and share them. Again, if you need more room, use your journal.

_____

_____

_____

_____

_____

_____

_____

CHAPTER TWENTY-SEVEN

ACTIVATE HEALING

"I have put my words in your mouth and covered you with the shadow of my hand—I who set the heavens in place, who laid the foundations of the earth, and who say to Zion, 'You are my people.'"

ISAIAH 51:16

In the last few chapters, I've shared with you what has been a successful battle strategy as the Lord and I have fought fear together and won, praise the name of Jesus. Now it is time to exchange our pain for the peace and healing paid in full for us by our Lord and Savior Jesus. In this final section of our *Fear Not!* journey together, we are doing a deep-dive into the inner recesses of your heart and mind. So get your tissues, a glass of water, and be prepared to spend all the time needed for this step. But let's first take a moment to pray:

"Almighty, All-Knowing Holy Creator, Abba God, thank you for this time together of healing. Jesus, thank you for providing healing for us by your more-than-enough sacrifice on the cross. Holy Spirit, we ask you to engage with us, enter this scene, and manifest your presence in holy, healing ways. Work in us and through us to completely deliver us from fear, anxiety, oppression, and depression, all the works of the enemy. We pray this in Jesus's almighty name, amen!"

Okay, as I promised earlier, we are now ready to **activate healing**. A critical part of our healing is freeing ourselves from any spirit of fear, oppression, depression, anxiety, bitterness, woundedness, pain, grief, or confusion that may have taken root. We are going to eradicate the works of the enemy from our lives so we can live more abundantly the life Jesus purchased, amen? But to remain free, we need Jesus in our lives. To maintain our liberty and authority over the devil, we need the blood of Jesus. So if you haven't yet received Jesus as your Lord and Savior, now is the time to do it.

Forgiveness

How then do we activate healing? It begins with one crucial step. In sharing my battle strategy, I haven't mentioned one very important element. I left this vital element until the very end because it is sometimes the hardest step. That step is forgiveness.

God reminded me of the importance of this step and gave me a promise regarding forgiveness through a dream I experienced right at the tail-end of my panic attack season. In the dream, it was a bright, beautiful day. I was striding forward into this gorgeous day, hurray! Unfortunately, I was dragging a boulder behind me that was bigger than I was. In my dream, the boulder had a name: Bitterness. Though I was working hard to move forward, I wasn't making much progress. When I looked closer, I realized the tethering rope was sinew from my own body.

I was pondering what it meant that my very own flesh had attached me to this giant boulder when a raven swooped in out of nowhere and landed on the boulder. It cocked its head this way and that, sizing up the sinew. Then quick as a wink, it opened its beak and bit the sinew in two, severing the boulder from me and me from the boulder. Maybe that sounds rather repulsive, but in my dream it all made sense. God's message in this dream was clear. Move forward and sever the past. All the injury, trauma, and rejection—cut it off forever. Sever once and for all the connection to that boulder of bitterness and unforgiveness.

The imagery in my dream of a boulder is interesting because many of us believe we've already forgiven. I certainly thought I had. But if we're still angry and resentful toward the wrong-doer or if painful memories keep cropping up, we haven't completely severed the bitterness boulder. This is a step we may need to revisit several times before receiving complete release.

You will know you are released from the bitterness boulder when you can remember the people or incidents that injured you so much but without the feelings of pain, anguish, hatred, or fear. The memories may not go away. They are a permanent part of your testimony. But the negative feelings about the memories will be replaced with peace and promise of a good future. That, my friend, is freedom!

In order to defeat the devil completely, we are going to have to forgive the person or people who caused the pain, trauma, or injury in our lives. Forgiving is a serious, deliberate choice, especially if forgiveness has not been requested by the injuring person. But when we choose to forgive, we release a prisoner. That prisoner is actually us as in the Matthew West gospel song "Forgiveness." Unforgiveness and bitterness can easily kick wide open the window of opportunity for a spirit of fear, anxiety, and depression, so we need to slam that window shut. Forgiveness is the most powerful freedom choice you can make, ever. Do it! You will never regret it.

Now that we've applied our battle strategy and taken the final urgent step of forgiveness, we can activate healing over your life with all its pains and traumas. We're going to do this praying together for God's healing and empowerment over each part of your life separately.

Healing and Empowerment for Heart and Soul

Turn back to the activities on identifying learned and inherited fears at the beginning of this book (Activities A and B). Spend some time reviewing them. Put yourself back in the situations you listed and remember the people involved. Recall how you were impacted and what behaviors and thinking patterns you see in yourself today that have resulted (whether directly or indirectly) from these events (see Activity D).

Once you've reviewed each scenario thoroughly, we are going to take several minutes to pray. We are going to lift Jesus up over these injuries, traumas, hurts, anger, and fears. We are going to pray for healing. This first prayer is so important because it releases any authority or jurisdiction the enemy may have over your life. Place your hand over your heart and pray this prayer with me out loud:

"Abba Father, I am sorry for the inaccurate identity I've carried in my heart and mind about myself. I repent for allowing the wrong identity to speak louder than the blood of Jesus. My true identity is that of your child whom you so loved that you purchased my righteous identity with the sacrifice of your Son. I am sorry that I've allowed my wounded self to wound others with the hurtful words I've spoken out. Please forgive me and reverse the damage and heal the wounds I've inflicted on others in Jesus's precious and holy name, I pray. Amen!"

Now we will apply the blood and resurrection power of Jesus. Pray this with me out loud:

"Jesus my Savior, I apply the peace and healing you purchased for me at the whipping post and on the cross. You fully paid for my freedom from disease and grief. Isaiah 53:5 says you were wounded [pierced through] for my transgressions, bruised [crushed] for my iniquities. You bore my sorrows [pain], and by your stripes [blows that cut in] I am healed. I apply your blood over my wounded heart and soul, Jesus. I receive the resurrection power you freely give and apply it to my heart and soul, Lord Jesus. My heart and soul are filled with your wonder-working resurrection power, making me whole and mighty. With your resurrection power, Jesus, I forgive the people who have hurt me [name them out loud]. I release them and sever any wounding soul ties they may have created in Jesus's mighty name. My identity is renewed, my peace restored, and my love for living for you is resuscitated, all for your glory, Jesus. Amen!"

Healing and Empowerment for the Mind

Now place your hand on the right side of your head and pray with me aloud:

"Lord Jesus, I apply your healing blood to my mind that it may be made whole and receive the peace purchased by Christ Jesus. Flashbacks, PTSD, anxiety disorder, hypertension, and chemical surges, go NOW in Jesus's name! Brain, thyroid, endocrine system, and immune system be healed in Jesus's name. I command all autoimmune disorders, inflammation, and chronic pain to be healed NOW in Jesus's name. I command this workmanship of God, this holy temple of the Living God, to be made completely whole in Jesus's name. Power of the Holy Risen One, be made manifest in my body for your glory in Jesus's name."

Resurrection Power for Life

Place your hand over your heart again and pray with me out loud:

"Abba, Daddy God, Creator of All, thank you for your redemption plan in Jesus Christ. I receive in my heart all that Jesus paid. May the Holy Lamb of God receive his full reward in this heart and in this life. Heart, be renewed. Joy, be restored. Life, be resuscitated. Time, be redeemed. Beauty for ashes. Dancing for sorrow. *Dunamis* power in place of defeat. Baptize this heart in your great love, Father, for the glory of your Son Jesus and the advancement of your kingdom on this earth in Jesus's name."

Evict the Evil One

Now, we are going to evict any hold the enemy has over your life. Together aloud, let's pray:

"Almighty, all-powerful Savior Jesus. Thank you for purchasing my peace and healing for every circumstance and disease. Thank you, Holy Spirit, for partnering with me to ensure that all Jesus purchased for me is fulfilled in me and that my Lord and Savior receives his full reward for his overpayment for my sin, sickness, and suffering. With the power and authority ensured by Jesus's scourge, crucifixion, death, and resurrection, I command the spirit of fear, depression, oppression, anxiety, bitterness, grief, confusion, and infirmity to leave me now in Jesus's name. Do not enter me again. Do not enter anyone or any living being around me or my family members or friends. In Jesus's name, go to dry uninhabitable places."

As you complete this prayer, you may feel physical manifestations in your body such as coughing, yawning, vomiting, or vocalizing. Don't be surprised or concerned. It's just the sign of the enemy's stronghold being released and his work being evicted from your life, praise God! Repeat this prayer until you feel release and peace.

Let's remain here for a few moments. Take a deep breath, breathing in the Holy Spirit who is all around us now. Then let the breath out, breathing out the works of the enemy. Let's do this a few times. In with the Holy Spirit and out with the enemy's devices. Hallelujah! Now let's continue to pray out loud, in the Spirit if possible. Continue praying until you feel released to move on.

Let's pray to cover any other details we don't know of, aren't aware of, or simply don't know how to pray for. Pray in the Spirit if possible. Continue until you feel released to stop. Over time, the Lord will reveal other areas in your emotions, thinking, and history that he wants you to release to him. God is a powerful gentleman. He doesn't want to crush you with weightiness, guilt, or condemnation. If you've been through a lot of trauma, he will likely work gently with you over time to release all the pain and strongholds to him.

Free for Life

Now check this out! You've just followed the Great Commission Jesus gave his disciples. You've just set a captive free. That's you! Now let's remain free. In order to remain in victory over the enemy, Jesus must be Lord and Savior in our lives. If you've never asked Jesus to be your Lord and Savior, let's do that now. Pray this out loud:

"Jesus, thank you for fully paying the price for my sickness, sin, and death. I am a sinner by human nature, but today I receive new life and a new nature in you. Please take all of my heart, my mind, my soul, and my life. Completely overtake me and be my Lord and Savior. Precious Jesus, it's in your name I pray, AMEN!"

CHAPTER TWENTY-EIGHT

FREEDOM AND WHOLENESS

"Praise be to the Lord, who has not let us be torn by their teeth. We have escaped like a bird from the fowler's snare; the snare has been broken, and we have escaped. Our help is in the name of the Lord, the Maker of heaven and earth."

PSALMS 124:6-8

"It is for freedom that Christ has set us free. Stand firm, then, and do not let yourselves be burdened again by a yoke of slavery."

GALATIANS 5:1

We are now at the end of my journey (at least to date) and the beginning of yours (at least from this point). I've shared my life story, my fears, and my testimony of God's redemptive grace in my life. We've laid out together a battle strategy against fear and prayed together to activate healing in your life.

So where do we go from here? Let me give just a few suggestions that have proved helpful in my own life as we close the pages of this journey together and you begin—or continue—your own walk out of bondage and fear.

First, don't lose sight of your true identity, purpose, and inheritance as a son or daughter of God. There is a New Testament verse from the apostle Peter's first epistle that I have memorized because it sums up so well these three elements.

> But you are a chosen race, a royal priesthood, a holy nation, a people for God's own possession, so that you may proclaim the excellencies of Him who has called you out of darkness into His marvelous light. (1 Peter 2:9, NASB)

Wow, did you get all that? We once lived in darkness. Now we live in God's marvelous light. Who are we? We are God's personal possession, people, nation, race. We are chosen, royal, holy. What is our purpose? To proclaim to a world that needs this good news how excellent and wonderful our heavenly Daddy is. To offer up continual offerings of praise and worship and spiritual sacrifices (1 Peter 2:5) as God's own appointed priesthood. And that's just from one verse.

Repeat this verse regularly to remind yourself of who you are to your heavenly Father. Go back and review the sections of this book on your identity, purpose, and inheritance, stating out loud what and who Scripture says you are.

Second, keep reviewing your battle strategy. Repeat the prayers and life-giving scriptures in this book until you are empowered. When you begin to feel defeated or difficult situations and seasons arise, review your battle plan again. Repeat the prayers again and keep reviewing until they are second nature.

Third, conduct a monthly maintenance for empowerment. Dust this book off every month (and the accompanying journal if you created one) and review your notes, battle plans, and promises from God. Sooner rather than later you will begin to rely on the grace, truth, and the very presence of Jesus more and more. His presence in your life will reshape you into someone you barely recognize. Hallelujah, you gorgeous creation of God!

Fourth, keep getting God's Word into your spirit. We feed our bodies several times a day to stay healthy. The Bible tells us that God's words are "life to those who find them and healing to all their flesh" (Proverbs 4:22). So we need to commit ourselves to feed our souls and spirits a life-giving, healthy diet of God's Word.

Fifth, share your testimony. The powerful impact of your testimony is something that cannot be denied. You are the star and key witness to your own incredible spiritual journey. You and your testimony are kingdom treasure. Combined, you have a heavenly mandate, power, and authority to replicate what has happened in your life into other lives. Your testimony is a sneak peek at God's own agenda and sets a precedent of what God is planning to do in and through you. Sharing your testimony builds faith and activates the move of God so that others will follow suit just as you did and move into their true destiny.

Thwarting the Thief's Sneak-Attack

This section is not so much advice or prophecy over you but just a heads-up to the devil's lying, scheming ways. The enemy will undoubtedly try to tempt you again with bitterness, unforgiveness, fear, anxiety, depression, and so on by recalling certain memories to your thoughts and/or dreams. Satan is an artist at camouflage. He will absolutely try to make it seem like it's not him by disguising his voice as yours and leaking little "thoughts" in your ear such as:

- Too bad you are so helpless, stupid, inadequate (fill in the blank); there's no way your future will be any different than your present.
- Why can't you just make a decision and stick with it? What a loser!
- Things aren't going to change; you were born a loser, and you'll always be one.
- If you were smarter, richer, better-looking, kinder, funnier, more interesting, a better speaker, had different skin color, hair color, height, weight (fill in the blank), *that* (fill in the blank) would have never happened to you.
- Look at her/him/them; they never appreciated you, still haven't learned to see your value, and probably never will.

Do not come into agreement with these lies of Satan! Instead, you are going to tell the enemy: "No, devil, I rebuke you in Jesus's name. The Holy Spirit of Jesus lives here, and there is no place for you. I am alive in Christ Jesus, and he is alive in me! There is life-creating, miracle-working, resurrecting power flowing through my veins because I'm a child of God."

The Bible says, "Resist the devil and he *will* flee" (James 4:7). Soon the devil will realize that you are serious and he is defeated. His taunts will become fewer and fewer. If he ever does taunt again with anxiety or fear, you will know what to do.

Never Buy into the Lies

Write down any other lies that come to mind over the next several months (see activity at the end of this chapter). Rebuke the devil for each and every thought and lie. Try not to spend time rehearsing or dwelling on them. Remembering detail is not the purpose of this exercise. The purpose is to grab those lies that try to exalt themselves above the name of Jesus in whose image you are created (2 Corinthians 10:4) and yank them up by the roots.

Follow up each lie with a truth about you as a son or daughter of God. Write down and speak out who you are in Christ Jesus. Review the Identity section of this book and find some verses that speak into your spirit. Highlight them. Underline them. Copy them on Post-It notes and put them on your mirrors and refrigerator. Keep these truths in front of your eyes, heart, and mind.

Remember that God's words are truth even when the circumstances around us don't align. Truth trumps facts. The promises in the Bible supersede the reality we experience in this temporal, temporary world.

Make Your First Love First Priority

God is love. God is perfect love. Tormenting fear comes from the devil. God gives us power, love, and a sound mind established on God's love.

> Fear not, little flock, for the Father has chosen gladly
> to give you the kingdom. (Luke 12:32)

Did you get that? You are chosen! You are SO loved! All promises in him are yes and amen (2 Corinthians 1:20). Life and life more abundantly—nothing missing, nothing broken—is his will for you (John 10:10).

In practice, I spend time with the Lover of my soul each morning. Sometimes I get to have more time, sometimes less. Throughout the day, however, even when my hands are busy, I can redirect my mind and heart to my one true Love. He is in me, and I am in him, always.

Here's a fun observation I've noticed lately. The Holy Spirit gives me the greatest ideas in the middle of spin class at the gym. It's crazy loud with thumping secular music. I'm hot and gasping for breath. But somewhere in that class my spirit checks out of the classroom and into the Holy Spirit's presence. And we have the best, most creative time together. So awesome! Now that's our God! He is incredible and always amazing, and he meets us right where we are.

Whether you are on your A-game today or back to struggling with old, resistant tendencies or even addictions, turn your attention to him. He is right there with you and will never turn away. There are many scripture verses that carry that promise. Even if our mother and father abandon us, he never will leave us nor forsake us (Psalms 27:10, Isaiah 49:15, Jeremiah 31:20).

ACTIVITY R: Truth or Lie

We can't be in worry and fear and resting in God's promises at the same time. Don't believe lies when God's Word tells the truth. To help combat the lies and replace them with the truth, I invite you to journal them below. Each time the enemy tries to throw a fiery dart of lies at you, document the date, rebuke the devil, and cloak yourself in the truth. First list what lie you are hearing. Then list what God's Word says about you. If you aren't sure about the latter, read back through the many scriptures in this book. Soon you will find that the same lie occurs less and less frequently until it is no longer a threat. If you need more room, use your journal.

Date: _____

Lie: _____

Truth: _____

Date: _____

Lie: _____

Truth: _____

Date: _____

Lie: _____

Truth: _____

EPILOGUE

Before we say goodbye (at least for now!), I want to thank you from the bottom of my heart for embarking with me on this incredible discovery of who we are in Christ Jesus—*more than conquerors!* What an honor and privilege it has been to journey with you.

I also want to encourage us both to never give up and give way to fear. We might falter sometimes. When we do, let's pick this book back up, pull out a promise, and brace back up on it. We *can* do this! We can live free of worry, depression, anxiety, and oppression because Jesus paid the price in full for our freedom. Through his sacrifice, we have been preauthorized and preordained to win this battle since God stood on the foundation of creation.

But there is even more great news to take away with us. We read earlier the words of Jesus to his disciples on his very last night with them, promising that those who believed in him would do even greater things than he did on this earth. All we have to do is ask with faith in the name of Jesus.

> Very truly I tell you, **whoever believes in me** will do the works I have been doing, and they **will do even greater things than these**, because I am going to the Father. And I will do whatever you ask in my name, so that the Father may be glorified in the Son. You may **ask me for anything in my name, and I will do it**. (John 14:12-14)

Do you believe that now? Do you also believe now that God sees all and knows all, is surprised by nothing, and has a glorious plan and purpose for your life? God thought of you as he was forming all of creation. He planned when you'd be born and the exact purpose and destiny for which he was creating you. He equipped you with all the gifts, strengths, and talents necessary to carry out his vision for you. He has administered healing, purpose, and promise to you with his very own Spirit-self.

You are treasured and adored by the Most High, the Creator of All. And he has great, extraordinary plans for your life. Plans of prosperity and blessings, great adventure, and super-good things that exceed your wildest dreams. In fulfilling his plans and purpose for your life, you will discover unspeakable joy.

If this seems too incredibly wonderful to accept as true, then spend some time asking the Lord what he thinks of you. Ask him, according to your destiny, what name he calls you. Ask him what he dreamed and planned for your life at the foundation of creation.

Then go dream with him. The Holy Spirit will show you what doors to walk through next. Be excited about what's coming next. Your greatest days are not behind you. They are straight out in front of you and not far away.

I'd like to invite you to join me in one last challenge. It's a big one. One that I am practicing daily, and I'll admit I don't always succeed. But here it is. Let's choose to walk in continual forgiveness for ourselves and for others, free of resentment and bitterness, free of plots of retaliation, free of reasoning and figuring out the whys and hows. I know this is wildly ambitious, but I believe it can be done. Do you?

If you'd like to take this challenge, begin by writing down a plan either in a new journal or notes on your phone. Create a success strategy. Add an accountability partner in your plan. Choose a trusted person to help you adhere to the plan. Take note of the wins. Take note of the losses and how those can be converted to wins.

I'm going to do this for a minimum of six months. Will you join me? If so, I'd be delighted to hear from you. Just drop me a note at *prayer@greaterthingstoday.com*. I would love to pray for you and/or share more about your journey and mine. And for more messages like these, visit me at *www.greaterthingstoday.com*.

I pray we will meet again, whether this side of heaven's gates or in our Savior's presence, whether in the pages of another book, virtually through electronic communication, verbally, or in person.

EPILOGUE

Until we do, know this. YOU ARE MORE THAN A CONQUEROR THROUGH HIM WHO LOVES YOU (Romans 8:37)!!!

May you enjoy a lifetime of peace, purpose, joy, and lavish blessings in Jesus's name!

In our Almighty Daddy's love,
Ami Thomson

Printed in the United States
by Bookmasters

Printed in the United States
By Bookmasters